Queen Victoria;

QUEEN VICTORIA

BY

RICHARD R. HOLMES, F.S.A.

LIBRARIAN TO THE QUEEN

BOUSSOD, VALADON & CO.,

303 FIFTH AVENUE,

NEW YORK.

QUEEN VICTORIA

BY

RICHARD R. HOLMES, F.S.A.

LIBRARIAN TO THE QUEEN

BOUSSOD, VALADON & CO.,

303 FIFTH AVENUE,

NEW YORK

LOUIS WEISS & CO., Printers,
116 Fulton Street,
New York.

PREFACE

Some explanation seems to be due as to the origin of this biography, and as to the form which it has assumed.

At the end of 1896 I was asked by the Publishers, Messrs. Boussod, Valadon & Co., to write for them a biography of the Queen, which should be illustrated by pictures from the Royal Collections. As Librarian at Windsor Castle, I could not undertake the task without first asking and obtaining the permission of Her Majesty.

Many little fables have from time to time grown up respecting the early life of Queen Victoria. It seemed, therefore, desirable to take this opportunity of correcting these inaccuracies, and, with this object, Her Majesty most graciously consented to supply notes on her childhood and youth, and at the same time to correct matters of fact, especially in reference to the period before her accession to the throne, and more generally, throughout the volume.

I am therefore, enabled to present, for the first time, an accurate account of the childhood and youth of Queen Victoria.

For the remainder of the work I have depended on records already accessible to the general public, and especially on Her Majesty's published journals, and Sir Theodore Martin's *Life of the Prince Consort.* I desire also to express my deep obligation to Mr. Rowland Prothero, who has, on behalf of Her Majesty read the proofs, and to whom I am indebted on every page of this biography.

The pictures contained in the volume are not drawn from the political, naval, or military history of the eventful and glorious reign of Queen Victoria. They rather illustrated Her Majesty's domestic life, and it, therefore, seemed to me more fitting that the accompanying biography should, in the main, deal with personal, and not with public events. For the selection of these illustrations my thanks are due to Mr. D. C. Thompson.

In conclusion, I take the opportunity of reiterating the explanatory statement made by me in a letter to the *Times,* published on March 26th, 1897. For the plan of the work, its scope, the selection of the details, and the form in which they are presented, I am alone responsible.

RICHARD R. HOLMES.

Windsor Castle,
  September 1st, 1897.

QUEEN VICTORIA.

CHAPTER ONE.

ANCESTRY OF THE QUEEN.

Victoria, Queen and Empress, holds her unique position among the Soverigns of Great Britain not solely on
account of the duration of her reign. Her Majesty,
alone among the Queens Regnant who have preceded
her, has been blessed with direct heirs. On three previous occasions the sceptre has been held by female
hands, and on each, at the death of the holder, the direct
line of succession has been interrupted. Mary, the elder
daughter of Henry VIII., who, after a short and troubled
reign, died in 1558, left no issue by her husband, Philip
of Spain. Under her successor, her half-sister Elizabeth,
the English nation freed itself from the domination of
Rome, crushed the power of Spain, laid the foundations
of empire beyond the seas, and produced a literature
which is the glory of our language. But Elizabeth died
unmarried. At her death the direct line of the house of
Tudor came to an end. The succession passed to the
house of Stuart, through the marriage of Margaret,
daughter of Henry VII., with James IV. of Scotland;
and her great-grandson, James VI. of Scotland, the son
of Elizabeth's rival, Mary, Queen of Scots, succeeded to

the English throne. With the death of Queen Anne, the dynasty of the Stuarts, after giving four kings and two queens to the list of English Sovereigns, terminated. Anne's elder sister, Mary, had indeed enjoyed the title of Queen, but she shared the throne with her husband, William of Orange, who survived her. On William's death Anne became sole monarch, and proved to be the last Queen Regnant till the present reign. Her rule, like that of Elizabeth, was distinguished for triumphs both in peace and war, as well as for brilliancy in literature. By her marriage with George, Prince of Denmark, the promise of direct heirs was frequent; but of all her children one only, William, Duke of Gloucester, lived long enough to make the direct succession probable, and, at the age of eleven, he, too, sickened and died. Direct heirs of James II. did indeed exist, but their claim to the Crown was debarred by the Act of Settlement of 1701, which confined the succession to Sophia, Electress Dowager of Hanover, and her successors, being Protestants.

Sophia, Electress of Hanover, was the twelfth child and youngest daughter of Frederick V., Elector Palatine and King of Bohemia, and of Elizabeth, daughter of James I. of England and VI. of Scotland. Born in 1630, at The Hague, when the fortunes of her parents were at their lowest ebb, her own fortunes were as changeable, though in an inverse manner. Her memoirs give an interesting picture of her life at The Hague in her early years, and of the manners and intrigues of the exiled English Court. From her cousin, Charles, Prince of Wales, and afterwards King, she attracted much attention, and by many of the Royalists it was both believed and hoped that she would become their future sovereign. In the Royal Library at Windsor is preserved a curious memento of this passage in her life. It is a copy of a very early edition of the " Eikon Basilike," in which the young King, not liking the coarsely executed portrait of himself bound up in the volume, has attempted to soften its features by touches of a pen. These not proving satisfactory, he has inserted another and more pleasing engraving of himself, on the back of which he has written, " For the Princess Sophia." The young Princess, however, had strength of mind to resist the advances of the Prince, and obtained permission to leave The Hague. Several suitors for her hand appeared, and at length, shortly after the Restoration, she became the wife of Duke Ernest of Brunswick-Luneburg, afterwards Elector of Hanover. To him she proved an attached and faithful wife till his death in 1698. Sprightly, clever, and intelligent in her youth, she retained throughout her long life her powers of mind. A warm admirer and correspondent of Descartes, she was also a close and intimate friend of Leibnitz, who was her constant visitor at Herrenhausen, where she relieved her studies in philososphy by the care she bestowed upon her gardens. In 1701 the Act of Settlement placed her next in succession to the Crown, which forty years before had been within her reach. But she died in the lifetime of Queen Anne, at whose death, a few weeks later, her son George, Elector of Hanover, was summoned to the vacant throne. Besides this Prince, the Electress Sophia had five other sons. Her only daughter, Sophia Charlotte, who married Frederick I., King of Prussia, and was mother of Frederick the Great, was a strong-minded and amiable princess, and had no small share in forming the character of the Princess Caroline of Anspach, of whom mention will be made presently.

In writing the life of a Queen whose personal influence upon her time has been so extraordinary, it is natural to pay some attention to those female members of her ancestry who, though not themselves Queens Regnant, have influenced the course of events during their lives, and have transmitted to their descendants unmistakable traces of their personality.

Margaret Tudor, through whom the blood of the earlier kings descends to the present race, bore a decided resemblance to her brother, Henry VIII. Impetuous, fond of power and loving display, she yet exhibited great firmness and capacity in the troublous times which succeeded the death of her husband at Flodden, as well as in the guardianship of his son, James V.

To the romantic and eventful life of her granddaughter, Mary Queen of Scots, her complex character and tragic fate, a whole literature has been dedicated. No personage in history has commanded more potent advocacy or been assailed by fiercer criticism. Born in 1542, she became Queen of Scotland at her father's death at the close of the same year. Before six years had elapsed she was sent to France, as the betrothed bride of the Dauphin, afterward Francis II. There she was educated, and her abilities, naturally great, were carefully developed. Her religious instruction was superintended with even more solicitude, for, as Queen of Scotland and a claimant to the throne of England, the hopes of Catholicism, and of the return of the British Islands to the supremacy of Rome rested upon her. She was married to Francis in April, 1556, and, on the death of Mary of England in November of the same year, she laid formal claim to the English throne in right of her descent from Henry VII., alleging as ground for her conduct the illegitimacy of Elizabeth; and, notwithstanding that the latter was declared Queen without opposition, Mary and her husband assumed, and after their succession to the French throne, on the death of Henry II. in 1559, continued to use, the titles of King and Queen of England, Scotland, and Ireland. This was the beginning of the bitter and lifelong animosity between the rival Queens.

At the close of 1560, a few days before she was eighteen years of age, Mary Stuart's husband died. Her career in France was over; her rule over Scotland was but nominal, and her own religion was there proscribed. Still, after much hesitation, she ventured to return, and on the 18th of August, 1561, landed at Leith. After this, her marriages, her romantic friendships, her battles, successes and defeats, her imprisonment and escapes, her flight from her kingdom, her lonely captivity and final trial and execution, have been inexhaustible themes for poets, painters, and dramatists of every land. They are universally known; and it is unnecessary here to give even the merest outline of her history, particularly as the first volume of the series of historical works, of which the present volume forms a part, has been devoted to an exhaustive discussion of the subject, and the second contains the history of her great rival Queen Elizabeth, the two representing, from opposite points of view, the struggles of Catholicism and Protestantism for ascendancy in this kingdom. With the death of Mary the last hope of the revival of the domination of Rome departed.

The consort of her son, James I. of England, the Princess Anne, was the second daughter of Frederick II. of Denmark and Sophia, of the House of Mecklenburg. By her mother, who was a highly accomplished woman, skilled in astronomy, chemistry and other sciences, the future Queen was educated with the greatest care. A lively temperament, and a quick and cultured intelligence were not the only charms of the Queen. She added to these the personal attractions of fine features and a brilliant complexion. It was from her that the Stuart family derived the features which are so familiar in the portraits of Henry, Prince of Wales, and of Charles I. and his descendants—a type so persistent and remarkable that, as Mr. Lang records in his latest work, describing Charles Edward Stuart in his youth, "A distinguished artists who outlined Charles's profile, and applied it to another of Her present Majesty in her youth, tells me that they are almost exact counterparts." In politics Anne took little part; her tastes lay in other directions, and she is chiefly remembered by her connection with the history of the English stage, and by her patronage of Ben Jonson. She was a good wife and mother, and died beloved and respected by the nation.

The noble character, heroic courage, and bitter misfortunes of her daughter Elizabeth have surrounded her memory with an immortal halo of romance. Born in 1596, she accompanied her parents to England. There she was brought up in those principles of the Protestant religion, by her steady adherence to which she was the means of raising her descendants to her father's throne. In the pride of her youth and beauty she was married to the young Elector Palatine, Frederick V., a nephew of the famous warrior, Maurice, Prince of Orange. The alliance was universally popular, as it connected the English royal family with some of the chief Protestant Courts in Europe. For some years her married life at Heidelberg was happy and even splendid; but her husband's acceptance of the offer of the vacant Crown of Bohemia was the beginning of the series of difficulties which ended in the loss not only of that Crown, but of his ancient dominions in the Palatinate. The Princess died in England in 1662, leaving behind her a name, long revered by the nation as that of a martyr in the cause of the religion to which they were so firmly attached.

Caroline of Brandenburg-Anspach, wife of George II., is another ancestress of the Queen who can never be passed over or forgotten in the history of the dynasty. Born in 1683, she lost her father at an early age. The greater part of her childhood was passed at Dresden at the gay court of the Elector of Saxony, who had become the second husband of her mother. In 1696 another change in her life occurred. Left an orphan by her mother's death, she remained for some years with her guardian, Frederick, Elector of Brandenburg, afterwards King of Prussia, and his wife, Sophia Charlotte, daughter of the Electress Sophia of Hanover. Under the care of this highly gifted woman, the character of the young princess was molded. Firm in her adhesion to the Protestant religion, she refused the splendor of an alliance with the future Emperor Charles VI., because such a union would have necessitated a change of faith. In her resistance to the proposals made to her, she was encouraged by the old Electress, and by Leibnitz, who was thus intimately connected with three generations of the house, which has played so important a part in English history. By his means, and with the aid of the old Electress Sophia, her marriage with the hereditary Prince of Hanover was accomplished. Of the story of her after life it is not necessary here to speak. Of her character, and especially of her devotion and self-sacrifice, it is difficult to say too much. Literature and the arts found in her a discriminating patron. The excellence of her own artistic taste is proved by the fact that she decorated her sitting-room at Kensington with the drawings by Holbein of the ladies and nobles of the Court of Henry VIII., which, with the equally priceless volume of drawings by Leonardo da Vinci, had been recently discovered in a cupboard of the Palace, and with the miniature portraits by Cooper and others, which are still not the least valuable of the treasures of the Crown. Till her death she retained her beauty, and the marked type of her features is perpetuated in the great family resemblance which is so noticeable in her descendants to the present day.

Queen Charlotte, the wife of George III., and the grandmother of our Sovereign, was a devoted wife and mother, and strict in her ideas of duty. Though her features were irregular, her face was attractive from the brightness of her eyes, and the piquancy and animation of her expression. One inestimable boon she helped to confer on the British nation. At a period when laxity of morals was almost universally prevalent, she not only set a noble example of domestic virtue, but resolutely discountenanced vice in others. It was in no small degree owing to her influence that the Court of George III. became the purest in Europe.

Of the Kings of England, the Queen's ancestors, it would be superfluous to give any history or account in the limited pages of this volume.

CHAPTER TWO.

It was on the 6th of November, 1817, that the whole country heard with dismay of the tragic death of the Princess Charlotte of Wales, wife of Prince Leopold of Saxe-Coburg, and of her newborn infant. With that event the hope of a direct heir to the Regent, afterwards George IV., disappeared, and the succession to the throne was left among his younger brothers. Of these the eldest, Frederick, Duke of York, had been married more than sixteen years, and had no children. William, Duke of Clarence, the next in seniority, who succeeded his brother as King William IV., was married on the 11th of July, 1818. His first child by his wife, Princess Adelaide of Saxe-Meiningen, was born in 1819, two months before the Princess Victoria, and died on the day of her birth. One other child was born at the close of the next year, but, at the age of three months, she also died. Next to the Duke of Clarence came the Duke of Kent, the father of our Queen.

Edward Augustus, the fourth son of George III. and Queen Charlotte, was born on the 2d of November, 1767, at Buckingham House. In the same house, at the time of the Prince's birth, Edward, Duke of York, brother of the King, was lying in state preparatory to his funeral the day following. From his deceased uncle, the infant prince, who was christened on the 30th of the same month, received his first name. His early years were passed under the care and tuition of John Fisher, afterwards Canon of Windsor, and Bishop, successively, of Exeter and Salisbury. The influence of this exemplary Christian and distinguished scholar was apparent in the piety, and love of truth, which were marked features in the character of his pupil, whose fortitude and equanimity were severely tried in after life by injustice and misfortune. Destined for the career of a soldier, he was sent, at the age of eighteen, to Luneberg, in Hanover, to study for his profession under a military governor. An annuity of £6,000 had been provided for his maintenance, but his tutor, who thought of nothing except drill and avarice, treated his charge with extreme severity and parsimony. Not content with restricting his pocket-money to a weekly pittance, he intercepted the Prince's letters to his parents, and misrepresented his conduct by dscribing him as recklessly extravagant. As the Prince afterwards said: "Much of the estrangement between my royal parent and myself, much of the sorrow of my after life, may be ascribed to that most uncalled-for sojourn in the Electorate." There is no doubt that the ill-judged and severe treatment of his governor was the primary cause of the serious financial embarrassments which trouble the Prince throughout the whole of his life.

In May, 1786, the Prince was made a Colonel in the Army, and, shortly after, a Knight of the Garter. In the year following he was removed to Geneva. Thence, in June 1790, he returned to England, without permission from the King, hoping that, in a personal interview with his father, he might so state his grievances as to obtain some immediate relief from the burdens which pressed upon him. The King, however, was unplacable; he refused to see his son, ordered him to leave in a few days for Gibraltar, and only admitted him to his presence for a few minutes before his departure. But the Prince's visit was not entirely fruitless; at last he was free from his harsh governor, and his exile was alleviated by his appointment to the Colonelcy of the 7th Royal Fusiliers, then forming part of the garrison. On his conduct in this position many unfavorable criticisms have been passed. The strict ideas of military duty which had been instilled into him in Germany made him a stern disciplinarian, at a time when the utmost laxity prevailed among the garrison of the Rock. To the Prince's credit it should be added that he demanded from his subordinates no more than he practised himself. As in the discharge of public duties he set an example of care and diligence, so in private life he was a pattern of regularity and temperance. The opinion entertained of him by his own regiment may be learned from its privately printed records, where it is said: "At that time the discipline of the Army was greatly relaxed. The military code, it is true, allowed brutal severity to be used in correcting the private soldiers, but brutal severity has never been the means of raising and maintaining a brave and efficient army, unless it is only resorted to in the last extremity by men who performed their duty with rigid exactness, and were in all respects a pattern for those whom they commanded. So much, however, could not then be said of all ranks in the British Army. Great slackness existed, and when the young Duke of Kent attempted to exact a proper and honorable performance of his duty from each of his subordinates, his meas-

ures were received with great and ill-concealed disgust."
" His notions of discipline," says the Prince's biographer,
" rendered him unpopular with the men. Representations relative to the dissatisfaction prevalent in the Fusiliers were made at home, and the result was that His
Royal Highness was ordered to embark with his Regiment for America." His enemies, and the Prince had
many on the Rock, not all of the lowest order, were
striving to create discord between him and his Fusiliers.
But gradually the advantages of strictness in discipline
were recognized, and before the regiment left Gibraltar
the merits of the Colonel were appreciated, not only by
th 7th, but by the rest of the garrison.

During 1792 and 1793 the Duke remained at Quebec
in command of his regiment. In October of the latter
year he was promoted to the rank of Major-General, and
in December, at his own request, he received an appointment under Sir Charles Grey, who was then engaged
in the reduction of the French West India Islands. The
Prince took part in the capture of Martinique and Santa
Lucia, for which service he was mentioned in dispatches,
and received the thanks of Parliament. After the successful termination of the expedition he rejoined his regiment in Canada; but, in 1798, he was obliged to leave the
country on account of ill-health.

In 1799 His Royal Highness was created Duke of
Kent and Strathern, and Earl of Dublin. In the same
year he was gazetted Commander-in-Chief of the Forces
in North America; but, owing to the state of his health,
he was able to remain there little more than a year. In
1802 he was again dispatched to Gibraltar, on this occasion as Governor, with express instructions from the
Commander-in-Chief, his brother, the Duke of York,

to restore the discipline of that demoralized garrison. The means which the Duke of Kent considered it necessary to take, at great pecuniary loss to himself, for the accomplishment of this purpose, caused a mutiny among the troops, which was at last quelled, and discipline restored. The Duke, however, was recalled, and after his departure the garrison relapsed into its former condition. In 1805 the Duke was made a Field-Marshal. He was at this time living in comparative retirement near Ealing, taking, however, an active interest in movements of piety and philanthropy. But in 1815 he was compelled, by the state of his affairs, and the difficulty which he experienced in obtaining any assistance towards the relief of his embarrassments, to leave England, in order that, on the Continent, he might live in the simplest possible manner. It was while he was abroad that he first saw the widowed Princess of Leiningen, whom he afterwards married.

The Princess Victoria Mary Louisa, who thus became Duchess of Kent, was born at Coburg on the 17th of August, 1786. She was the fourth daughter of Francis Frederick Antony, Duke of Saxe-Coburg-Saalfield, and his wife, Augusta, daughter of Henry, Count of Reuss-Ebersdorf. When seventeen years of age, she had married Ernest Charles, Hereditary Prince of Leiningen, her senior by more than twenty years, and a widower, whose first wife, the Princess Sophie Henriette, had also been of the same house of Reuss-Ebersdorf. After eleven years of married life, she was left a widow, with two children—a son, Prince Charles, who succeeded his father in 1814, and a daughter, Princess Feodore, the beloved half-sister and companion of the girlhood of Queen Victoria. The Princess of Leiningen cordially returned

the affection with which she had inspired the Duke of
Kent, and when it was known that sanction had been
given to the Duke's marriage with the sister of Prince
Leopold, the intelligence was received everywhere with
the greatest satisfaction. It was a union which had been
most ardently desired by the Princess Charlotte, who
was deeply attached to her uncle. But, owing to the
delays which were occasioned by the position of the Princess of Leiningen as guardian of her two fatherless children, the Princess Charlotte's sudden death occurred before the alliance was concluded. The House of Commons voted a grant of £6,000 a year, and on the 29th of
May, 1818, the marriage of the Duke of Kent and the
Princess of Leiningen was celebrated at Coburg. The
ceremony was repeated on the 11th of June, at Kew,
and at the same time and place the Duke of Clarence
was married to the Princess Adelaide of Saxe-Meiningen.

For the first few months of their married life, the Duke
and Duchess of Kent resided at Amorbach, one of the
seats of the Prince of Leiningen. Early in the following
Spring, when the birth of their child was expected, both
the Duke and Duchess were desirous that the infant
should first see the light on English soil, and made their
way to Kensington. There, on the 24th of May, 1819,
the Princess, the future Queen and Empress, was born
at a quarter past four in the morning. Though the
Duchess quickly recovered her health, yet, towards the
close of the year, she was advised to try a climate somewhat milder than that of Kensington, as the Winter had
set in with such unusual severity that thick ice was everywhere to be seen as early as November. A move was
therefore made to Devonshire, where Woolbrook Cottage, at Sidmouth, was taken as a Winter residence.

Here the Duke passed the short remainder of his life, overshadowed to some extent by the clouds of financial trouble which had always so terribly oppressed him, but brightened by the affection and companionship of his wife, and of his child, to whom he was devotedly attached. His end was very sudden; he had walked out through the snow with Colonel Conroy, but on his return neglected to change his wet clothes. This imprudence, following on a cold which he had caught at Salisbury when visiting the Cathedral, brought on inflammation of the lungs. The fever ran high, and, according to the barbaric custom of the age, he was repeatedly bled. He never regained strength, and died on the 23d of January, 1820. During his illness, he was nursed indefatigably by the Duchess, who never left him; indeed, for five nights and days she had never undressed. The only consolation she had besides her infant daughter was the presence of her loved brother, Prince Leopold, who, on hearing of the dangerous condition of the Duke, hastened at once to her side. The Duke's sister, Princess Augusta, writes to an old friend immediately after the Duke's death: "Think, my dearest Lady Harcourt, that yesterday five weeks he was here on his way to Sidmouth; so happy with his excellent, good wife, and his lovely child; and within so short a time was perfectly well—ill—and no more! . . . God knows what is for the best, and I hope I bow with submission to this very severe trial; but when I think of his poor, miserable wife, and his innocent, fatherless child, it really breaks my heart. She has conducted herself like an angel, and I am thankful dearest Leopold was with her. . . . She quite adored poor Edward, and they were truly blessed in each other; but what an irreparable loss he must be to her!"

The Duke of Kent was also a loss to the whole nation. Not a favorite with his own family, he was the most popular of his brothers outside the Royal circle. His opinions were enlightened, and, though considered heterodox at the time, they now represent the views of most cultivated men. In his private life he was remarkable for his generosity to all from whom he had received attention or service. Warmly interested in the management of almost every charitable institution of his time, he never failed to forward their interests by presiding at their meetings if time would permit him to do so. The practical interest he took in education is proved by the fact that he was the first commander of a regiment to establish a regimental school. Perhaps the best eulogy cast upon him wah that of Lord Brougham, who said, in the House of Lords, on the question of a grant to him on his marriage, that he "would venture to say that no man had set a brighter example of public virtue, no man had more beneficially exerted himself in his high station to benefit every institution with which the best interests of the country, and the protection and education of the poor were connected, than His Royal Highness the Duke of Kent."

The Duke was buried in the royal vault at Windsor, under the Tomb-house, now the Albert Memorial Chapel. A handsome tomb of alabaster, with a recumbent effigy, has also been erected by the Queen to her father's memory in the south aisle of the nave of St. George's Chapel.

A week had not elapsed since the leath of the Duke before his father, George III., also passed away. The Princess Augusta again writes from Windsor Castle on the 4th of February: " In all my sorrow I cannot yet bear to think of that good, excellent woman, the Duchess of Kent, and all her trials; they are really most grievous. She is the most pious, good, resigned creature it is possible to describe. She has written to me once; and I received the letter from her and one from Adelaide, written together from Kensington. Dearest William is so good-hearted, that he has desired Adelaide to go to Kensington every day, as she is a comfort to the poor widow, and her sweet, gentle mind is of great use to the Duchess of Kent. It is a great delight to me to think they can read the same prayers, and talk the same mother tongue together, it makes them such real friends and comforts to each other. . . ."

This friendship with the Duchess of Clarence was real and lasting. It helped materially to soften the sorrows of the early days of the Duchess's widowhood, when, for the sake of her child, she resolved to remain permanently in the land of her adoption. After she lost her second Princess, the future Queen Adelaide wrote to the Duchess of Kent: "My children are dead; but yours lives, and she is mine too," and throughout the remainder of her life she treated her niece with an affection which was truly maternal. In addition to her other troubles, the royal widow was left in very straitened circumstances, and though for some time helped by the generosity of her brother, it was many years before any adequate provision was made for her maintenance.

Particular attention has been drawn in the previous chapter to the female members of the ancestry of the Queen in the male line. Here it is equally important to mention the great influence which the Queen's grandmother in the female line had upon her character and her life. She was, as is mentioned above, a Princess of the ancient house of Reuss-Ebersdorf. Her mother was of the house of Erbach-Schoenberg, which family has again, in recent years, been allied to the royal family of Great Britain by the marriage of the Count of Erbach-Schoenberg with the sister of the lamented Prince Henry of Battenberg. The Duchess of Coburg is described by her third and favorite son, the King of the Belgians, as being in every way " a most distinguished person," and the Queen, speaking of her many years later, thus records her recollections: " The Queen remembers her dear grandmother perfectly well. She was a most remarkable woman, with a most powerful, energetic, almost masculine mind, accompanied with great tenderness of heart and extreme love for nature. The Prince (Consort) told the Queen that she had wished earnestly that he should marry the Queen, and as she died when her grandchildren (the Prince and Queen) were only twelve years old, she could have little guessed what a blessing she was preparing, not only for this country, but for the world at large. She was adored by her children, particularly by her sons; King Leopold being her great favorite. She had fine and most expressive blue eyes, with the marked features and long nose inherited by most of her children and grandchildren." This note by the Queen, with several letters of this gifted lady, is printed in General Grey's " Early Years of the Prince Consort." The Dowager Duchess of Coburg died in 1831. The Queen believes that whatever powers of mind and talents she may possess are principally inherited from her maternal grandmother, of whom a characteristic portrait, from a miniature, is given opposite page 14.

The sisters of the Duchess of Kent, and aunts to the Queen, were Spohia, Antoinette, and Julie. Sophia, the eldest, after refusing many eligible proposals of marriage from suitors of her own rank, married in 1804 Count Mensdorff-Pouilly, whose acquaintance she had made when visiting her sister, Antoinette, at Fantaisie, near Baireuth, at that time the resort of many Bavarian families, as well as of French emigrants. The second daughter of the Duchess of Saxe-Coburg, Antoinette, married in 1798 Duke Alexander of Wurtemberg, whose sister, the Empress of Russia, was mother to the Emperors Alexander and Nicholas. The Duke Alexander held a very influential position in that country, where he resided many years. His wife is described by her brother, King Leopold, as clever, amiable, and possessed of a great esprit de conduite. They had two sons, both of whom served with distinction in the Russian Army; the elder married Princess Marie of Orleans, daughter of Louis Philippe, and their son, Duke Philip, is heir-presumptive to the throne of Wurtemberg. The third sister, Julie, was married at fifteen to the Grand Duke Constantine of Russia. The marriage was not happy, and in 1802 she left Russia, fixing her residence finally at Elfenau, near Berne, in Switzerland, where she was visited in 1837 by her nephew, Prince Albert, a visit repeated on more than one occasion afterwards.

CHAPTER THREE.

Conformably with the custom of the Church of England, the infant daughter of the Duke and Duchess had, as soon as possible after her birth, been baptized at Kensington Palace; the rite being administered by the Archbishop of Canterbury, who was assisted by the Bishop of London. The Prince Regent stood as sponsor, with the Duke of York, who represented the Emperor of Russia. The godmothers were the Duchess Dowager of Coburg, the maternal grandmother of the Princess, represented by the Duchess of Gloucester; and the Queen of Wurtemberg, Princess Royal of England, who was represented by her sister, the Princess Augusta. The names given were Alexandrina Victoria, the first after the Emperor of Russia, the second after her mother. For a short time the pet name of " Drina " was used, but later it was supeseded by the universally honored name of Victoria. One of the Queen's earliest signatures, in capital letters and in pencil, written by her when four years old, and using this name only, is in the British Museum.

Immediately after her father's death she was brought back, with her widowed mother, by Prince Leopold, from Sidmouth to Kensington, which was to be her future home till, by the death of her uncle, William IV., she succeeded to the throne. The Duchess of Kent in after years, in reply to an address of congratulation on the attainment of her majority by her daughter, has thus described the motives of her conduct in her new position: " I pass over the earlier part of my connection with this country. I will merely observe, that my late regretted consort's circumstances and my duties obliged us to reside in Germany; but the Duke of Kent, at much inconvenience, and I, at great personal risk, returned to England, that our child should be ' born and bred a Briton.' In a few months afterwards my infant and myself were awfully deprived of father and husband. We stood alone —almost friendless and alone in this country; I could not even speak the language of it. I did not hesitate how to act. I gave up my home, my kindred, my duties (the Regency of Leiningen), to devote myself to that duty which was to be the whole object of my future life. I was supported in the execution of my duties by the country. It placed its trust in me, and the Regency Bill gave me its last act of confidence. I have, in times of great difficulty, avoided all connection with any party in the State; but, if I have done so, I have never ceased to impress on my daughter her duties, so as to gain, by her conduct, the respect and affection of the people. This, I have taught her, should be her first earthly duty as a Constitutional Sovereign." No words could better convey a sense of the principles which guided the mother in the education of her child, and of the manner in which, not always without opposition, she fulfilled the task she had set before herself to perform.

For the first few years of her life at Kensington, then really a suburb—for London itself ended at Tyburn Gate and at Hyde Park Corner—the Duchess watched most carefully over the health and physical development of her daughter. Whenever the weather permitted the Princess was to be seen in the gardens, generally accompanied by her half-sister, the Princess Feodore, and in charge of her nurse, Mrs. Brock, whom she called her " dear, dear Bobby." Many stories are related of the manner in which the child would recognize any ladies of the neighborhood who happened to meet the royal party; but most of these, if they ever had any small foundation in fact, have been overlaid with exaggeration and the most improbable details. One instance of the manner in which what must have been a very trifling incident has grown in the telling, is the story related by an old soldier named Maloney, who claimed the honor of having saved his sovereign's life in her infancy. The pony drawing the chair in which the Princess took her morning ride, frightened by a dog, swerved, and overturned the chair on the edge of the pathway. The child would have fallen under the vehicle, when Maloney seized her in her fall, and was able to restore her unhurt to the lady attendant. The following day he received from the Duchess her thanks, with a guinea. The Queen has no recollection of this incident, and is sure she never was upset, or in any danger of being thrown out. In 1878 the circumstance was brought up again, and some assistance was given to the old man, who was in distress, though no proof of his claim could be discovered. The Queen's earliest recollection is that of crawling on the floor on an old yellow carpet at Kensington Palace, and playing with the badge of the Garter belonging to Bishop Fisher, who, as Bishop of Salisbury, was then Chancellor of the Order, and, having been tutor to her father, took a deep and affectionate interest in the welfare of the Duke's only child. Mr. Wilberforce, who was then living at Kensington Gore, describes to Hannah More a visit which he paid to the Duchess in July, 1820: " In consequence of a very civil letter from the Duchess of Kent, I waited on her this morning. She received me, with her fine, animated child on the floor by her side, with its playthings, of which I soon became one. She was very civil, but as she did not sit down, I did not think it right to stay above a quarter of an hour."

During these early years, and before a regular course of studies had been attempted, the family life at the Palace was simple and regular. Breakfast was served in Summer at eight o'clock, the Princess Victoria having her bread and milk and fruit on a little table by her mother's side. After breakfast the Princess Feodore studied with her governess, Miss Lehzen, and the Princess Victoria went out for a walk or drive. It has been repeatedly said that at this time she was instructed by her mother; but this is not the case, as the Duchess never gave her daughter any lessons. At two there was a plain dinner, when the Duchess had her luncheon. In the afternoon was the usual walk or drive. At the time of her mother's dinner the Princess had her supper laid at her side. At nine she was accustomed to retire to her bed, which was placed close to her mother's.

It has been said that on the Princess's fourth birth-day her uncle, King George, presented her with a splendid gift of a minature of himself set in diamonds. This is not the fact; at the Royal Lodge in Windsor Park, in 1827, the King presented the Princess with a badge, worn by the Royal Family, which is still preserved. Another tradition belonging to the same period runs that the King issued invitations for a State dinner, and signified his wish that her infant daughter should accompany the Duchess, and that the Princess was accordingly presented to the assembly before the banquet. This took place at the Carlton House, but the Princess was present only for a moment to see the King and the Royal Family.

It was not till the Princess had entered her fifth year, that she began to receive any regular instruction. On the recommendation of the Rev. Thomas Russell, Vicar of Kensington, the Rev. George Davys was engaged to give elementary lessons. In this determination not to force her daughter's mind, the Duchess of Kent acted on the counsel of her mother, who had advised her " not to tease her little puss with learning while she was so young." The advice was justified by results, for the Princess made rapid progress. In this year, 1824, the Duchess of Saxe-Coburg came over to England to visit her son, Prince Leopold, and the united family spent that Autumn at Claremont. Then, and for years afterwards, these visits to her loved uncle were some of the brightest remembrances of the Queen, who has written, " These were the happiest days of the Queen's childhood." Years afterwards, in 1842, when staying at Claremont with her husband and eldest child, the Queen wrote to her uncle Leopold at Brussels: " This place brings back recollections of the happiest days of my otherwise dull childhood—days when I experienced such kindness from you, dearest uncle; Victoria plays with my old bricks, and I see her running and jumping in the flower garden, as old (though I feel still little) Victoria of former days used to do."

About the same time, Miss Lehzen, the daughter of a Hanoverian clergyman, who had come over to England in charge of the Princess Feodore, was appointed governess to the Princess. She was her constant guide and companion and devotedly attached to her young charge, by whom the feeling was cordially returned. Her great influence was exercised with tact and judgment, and the bond of union between teacher and pupil was only severed by death. In recognition of her distinguished merit, Miss Lehzen was created a Baroness of Hanover by George IV. After the accession of her pupil to the throne, the Baroness remained with the Queen till her marriage. Two years later, she retired to Germany, and died, much regretted, in 1870.

In 1826, when the Princess was seven years old, she received, for the first time, an invitation from the King to accompany the Duchess of Kent on a visit to him at Windsor. His Majesty was then living in the Royal Lodge in the Park. As there was no accommodation for visitors in the Lodge, the Duchess and the Princess stayed at Cumberland Lodge, close at hand, where they remained for three days. The King was much pleased with his niece, and with the affection she exhibited towards himself. Before she left, he gave her the badge worn by members of the Royal Family and promised an early renewal of her visit to him—a promise afterwards fulfilled. The Princess thus for the first time had the opportunity of seeing the stately castle, which then, after a century's neglect, was being restored as a fitting abode for the Sovereign, and has for sixty years been her chief home of state.

One day, during her first visit to the Royal Lodge, the King entered the drawing-room, holding his niece by the hand. The band was playing in the adjoining conservatory. "Now, Victoria," said His Majesty, "the band is in the next room, and shall play any tune you please. What shall it be?" "Oh, Uncle King," quickly replied the Princess, "I should like 'God Save the King.'" Another time, His Majesty asked her what she had enjoyed most during her stay in Windsor. "The drive I took with you, Uncle King," was the answer, the King having himself driven her in his pony phaeton, in company with the Duchess of Gloucester.

The Earl of Albemarle, who was in attendance on the Duke of Sussex at Kensington, thus describes in his recollections the appearance of the Princess at this time: "One of my occupations on a morning, while waiting for the Duke, was to watch from the window the movements of a bright, pretty little girl, seven years of age. She was in the habit of watering the plants immediately under the window. It was amusing to see how impartially she divided the contents of the watering-pot between the flowers and her own little feet. Her simple but becoming dress contrasted favorably with the gorgeous apparel now worn by the little damsels of the rising generation—a large straw hat and a suit of white cotton; a colored fichu round the neck was the only ornament she wore."

The education of Her Royal Highness was now conducted on a regular system. Besides the instruction she received from Miss Lehzen and the Rev. George Davys, Mr. Steward, the writing master of Westminster School, was engaged to teach writing and arithmetic; Mr. J. B. Sale, who had been in the choir of the Chapel Royal, came to assist in the singing lessons, which were afterwards given by the famous Lablache. Lessons in dancing were given by Madame Bourdin, to whose teaching may be due in some measure the grace of gesture and dignity of bearing which has always distinguished Her Majesty. Drawing was intrusted to Mr. Westall, who had been a Royal Academician since 1794, and was now of considerable age; he carefully trained the great natural gifts of his pupil, who early showed a talent which, had there been sufficient time for its exercise in after years, would have placed its possessor in the first rank among amateur artists. The fac-simile of a drawing by the Princess is given at the end of this chapter; it is a copy from a design by her master, and is also interesting as being the last birthday present given by his niece to George IV.; on the back of it is written, in the King's hand, "Drawn by the Princess Victoria, and given to me by her, August 12th, 1829." The drawing is also dated and signed by the youthful artist.

At the time these various accomplishments were being taught, the Princess was well grounded in English, and knew something of French, which she studied under M. Grandineau. German was not allowed to be spoken; English was always insisted upon, though a knowledge of the German language was imparted by M. Barez. The lessons, however, which were the most enjoyed were those in riding, which has always been since one of the Queen's greatest pleasures.

In January, 1827, at the Duchess of Rutland's house in Arlington Street, the Duke of York died childless, bringing the Princess Victoria one step nearer to the throne. The stories which have been printed of the great attachment between uncle and niece, and of the constant visits paid to him by the Princess, are without foundation, as, in fact, the Queen never visited him till the last months of his life, when he was living at a house in King's Road, belonging to Mr. Greenwood, where

the Duke had " Punch and Ju'ly' to amuse the child.
In the year following, the Princess Feodore, who had
been her half-sister's constant companion, married
Prince Hohenlohe-Langenburg. This parting was the
greatest sorrow the Princess Victoria had then known,
as she missed her society not only at Kensington, but
even more in those visits to Ramsgate, Tunbridge Wells,
and other watering-places, which the Duchess was accustomed to pay with her family in the Summer months.

The death of the Duke of York, and the remote probability of the Duke and Duchess of Clarence having other
offspring, drew increasing attention to the movements
of the Duchess of Kent and her daughter. Many stories
are current of the behavior and appearance of the young
Princess. The simplicity of her tastes was particularly
noticed and admired. It was this simplicity of living
and careful training in home life which endeared not
only the Princess but her mother also to the hearts of
the whole nation. Leigh Hunt and Charles Knight have
both recorded the pleasing impression made upon them
by the young Princess. The latter, in his " Passages
of a Working Life," says: " I delighted to walk in
Kensington Gardens. As I passed along the broad central walk I saw a group on the lawn before the Palace.
. . . The Duchess of Kent and her daughter, whose
years then numbered nine, are breakfasting in the open
air. . . . What a beautiful characteristic it seemed
to me of the training of this royal girl, that she should
not have been taught to shrink from the public eye;
that she should not have been burdened with a premature conception of her probable high destiny; that she
should enjoy the freedom and simplicity of a child's
nature; that she should not be restrained when she starts

up from the breakfast-table and runs to gather a flower in the adjoining pasture; that her merry laugh should be as fearless as the notes of the thrush in the groves around her. I passed on and blessed her; and I thank God that I have lived to see the golden fruits of such a training."

Another and more celebrated writer, Sir Walter Scott, has written in his diary of May 19th, 1828: " Dined with the Duchess of Kent. Was very kindly received by Prince Leopold, and presented to the little Princess Victoria, the heir-apparent to the Crown, as things now stand. . . . This little lady is educated with much care, and watched so closely that no busy maid has a moment to whisper, ' You are heir of England.' I suspect, if we could dissect the little heart, we should find some pigeon or other bird of the air had carried the matter." Sir Walter's surmise, as will be seen later, was not altogether without foundation.

On the 28th of May, 1829, when the Princess was just ten years old, she made her first acquaintance with the ceremony of a court. This was at a juvenile ball, given by the King to Donna Maria La Gloria, Queen of Portugal (a sovereign only a month older than herself). The same year the Princess saw, for the last time, her uncle, George IV. Her grandmother, the Dowager Duchess of Coburg, mentions this visit to Windsor in a letter to the Duchess of Kent. " I see by the English papers that ' Her Royal Highness the Duchess of Kent went on Virginia Water with His Majesty.' The little monkey must have pleased and amused him, she is such a pretty, clever child."

This year the Summer was spent at Broadstairs, and, in returning to Kensington, a visit of two days was paid to the Earl of Winchilsea, at his seat, Eastwell Park, near Ashford.

The year 1830 was a momentous one in the life of the Princess. Her uncle George IV. died in June, and was succeeded by his brother William IV., this one life only now standing between her and the throne. The Princess, according to one account, already knew something of the position in which she was placed before the death of George IV. It is, however, certain that in the latter part of the year the Princess was formally acquainted with her position. The Baroness Lehzen, writing to Her Majesty on the 16th of December, 1867, thus describes the manner in which the communication was made: " I ask your Majesty's leave to cite some remarkable words of your Majesty's when only twelve years old, while the Regency Bill was in progress. I then said to the Duchess of Kent, that now, for the first time, your Majesty ought to know your place in the succession. Her Royal Highness agreed with me, and I put the genealogical table into the historical book. When Mr. Davys was gone, the Princess Victoria opened, as usual, the book again, and, seeing the additional paper, said: ' I never saw that before.' ' It was not thought necessary that you should, Princess,' I answered. 'I see, I am nearer the throne than I thought.' ' So it is, madam,' I said. After some moments the Princess resumed: ' Now, many a child would boast, but they don't know the difficulty. There is much splendor but there is more responsibility.' The Princess, having lifted up the forefinger of her right hand while she spoke, gave me that little hand, saying: ' I will be good. I understand now why you urged me so much to learn, even Latin. My aunts Augusta and Mary never did; but you told me

Latin is the foundation of English grammar, and of all the elegant expressions, and I learnt it as you wished it, but I understand all better now,' and the Princess gave me her hand, repeating, 'I will be good.' I then said: 'But your aunt Adelaide is still young, and may have children, and of course they would ascend the throne after their father, William IV., and not you, Princess.' The Princess answered: 'And if it was so, I should be very glad, for I know by the love Aunt Adelaide bears me, how fond she is of children.'"

This letter, written more than five-and-thirty years after the event, can hardly be considered as strictly accurate. The Princess was only eleven when the Regency Bill was discussed. It was passed in December, 1830. The Queen says, moreover, that the knowledge of her probable succession came to her gradually and made her very unhappy; nor does she feel sure that she made use of the expression, " I will be good."

Ampler provision had by this time been made for the maintainance of a houschold more in keeping with the recognized position of the Princess. It was consequently possible for the Duchess of Kent and her daughter to combine the pleasure of Summer travel with the increase of knowledge derived from wider association with the people which were hereafter to come under the Princess' rule. This year, therefore, a more extended journey was made. On the way to Malvern, where they were to spend a couple of months, visits were paid to Blenheim, also to Stratford-on-Avon, Warwick, Kenilworth, and Birmingham. Here the principal manufactures were seen, attention being particularly paid to the glass-blowing and coining. From Malvern excursions were made to Madresfield, Eastnor, and other noblemen's seats, and also to the cities of Hereford and Worcester. Returning from this pleasant sojourn in the west, both Badminton and Gloucester were visited, and the journey continued through Bath to Mr. Watson Taylor's, at East Stoke Park, where the acquaintance of Thomas Moore was made. In his diary we read: "The Duchess sang a duet or two with the Princess Victoria, and several very pretty German songs by herself. I also sang several songs with which Her Royal Highness was much pleased." The party thence passed over Salisbury Plain and visited Stonehenge on the way to Salisbury, where the young Princess was received with great enthusiasm, the horses being taken out of the carriage, which was drawn by the populace to the hotel.

The next stay was at Portsmouth, where the Princess visited the Royal George yacht and the St. Vincent man-of-war, and took a long survey of the dockyard, in which she was keenly interested.

The Regency Bill, just mentioned, was brought forward in the House of Lords by Lord Lyndhurst, in consequence of the reference made to the subject in the King's Speech from the Throne, on the 2d of November. It was introduced on the 15th of the month by the Lord Chancellor, who said: "The first question which your Lordships will naturally ask is—whom we propose as the guardian of Her Royal Highness under the circumstances inferred? I am sure, however, that the answer will at once suggest itself to every mind. It would be quite impossible that we should recommend any other individual for that high office than the illustrious Princess, the mother of Her Royal Highness the Princess Victoria. The manner in which Her Royal Highness, the Duchess of Kent, has hitherto discharged her duty

in the education of her illustrious offspring—and I speak
upon the subject, not from vague report, but from accurate information—gives us the best ground to hope most
favorably of Her Royal Highness' future conduct.
Looking at the past, it is evident we cannot find a better
guardian for the time to come." The Bill was passed
at the beginning of the next month. It provided that,
in the event of a posthumous child of the Queen Adelaide, Her Majesty should be guardian and regent during the minority of the infant. If that event should not
occur, the Duchess of Kent was to be guardian and regent during the minority of her daughter, the Princess
Victoria, the heiress presumptive. The provisions of
the Bill were welcomed and indorsed by the approval of
both Houses, and by the country at large. Every one
rejoiced in the opportunity of offering so worthy a tribute of gratitude to the royal lady for the unwearied as-
siduity and judgment she had displayed in the education
of her daughter for the station to which it seemed now
certain that she would eventually be called. It was on
the occasion of the prorogation of this session by the
King that the Princess Victoria was a witness of the
state procession, in company with the Queen and the
royal Princesses. The people cheered the Queen with
much vigor, whereupon that lady graciously took her
young niece by the hand, and, leading her to the front
of the balcony, introduced her to her future loyal subjects.

Soon after the King's accession, the Prime Minister,
Earl Grey, proposed to the Duchess of Kent, by the
King's desire, the appointment of a dignitary of the
Church to superintend the education of the Princess,
and suggested that the Bishop of Lincoln would be a

proper person to be intrusted with the duties of the office. The Duchess commissioned his Lordship to convey to the King her grateful thanks for the interest taken by him in the subject, and added that she perfectly coincided with His Majesty's views, as regarded the propriety of the establishment of the Princess being headed by a dignitary of the Church; but as she felt most perfect confidence in Mr. Davys, she thought there could be no difficulty in preferring him to an office of ecclesiastical dignity. Mr. Davys was, in consequence, in January, 1831, preferred to the Deanery of Chester.

Another important addition to the household of the Princess was made by the appointment of a State governess, in the person of Charlotte Florentia, daughter of the Earl of Powis, and wife of Hugh, third Duke of Northumberland. Her Grace had no share in the teaching of her charge, but was always in attendance when the heiress-presumptive appeared in public or at Court.

The Princess' first appearance at Court was at a Drawing Room held on the 24th of February, 1831, in honor of the birthday of Queen Adelaide. During the reception she stood on the left of the Queen, between one of her royal aunts and the Duchess of Kent, dressed very simply in white, with a pearl necklace, and a diamond ornament in her hair. She much enjoyed the ceremony, and henceforward attended the Drawing Rooms twice in the year, not attending any of the State Balls or ceremonies in the evening till some years later.

In August of this year the Duchess of Kent and the Princess went to the Isle of Wight, where they stayed for two months. The coronation of King William IV. was fixed for the 8th of September, and all preparations had been made for the attendance of the heiress-presumptive at the ceremony. The Duchess of Kent was expected at Claremont, and had appointed Lord Morpeth to be the bearer of her coronet to the Abbey. The absence of the royal pair from the Coronation gave rise at the time to much comment and angry discussion. During her stay in the island, the Princess made a tour round its western part, visiting Ryde, Ventnor, Yarmouth, and Newport, and returning home to pay a visit at Claremont to her uncle, King Leopold. He and the Duchess of Kent had, directly after this visit, to mourn the loss of their mother, the Duchess Dowager of Coburg, who had watched with such anxious care and solicitude over the welfare of her children and grandchildren, and had ardently desired, but never was destined, to see that union which afterwards, while it lasted, rendered the lives of two of them so blissful.

In the Summer of 1832 a somewhat lengthy tour was taken by the Duchess of Kent and the Princess, who thus had an opportunity of seeing a great extent of her future kingdom, and making the personal acquaintance of many of the nobility and gentry, and gaining an insight into the manufactures and employments of the people. Starting in the beginning of August and sleeping at Oxford, they passed through Birmingham, Wolverhampton, and Shrewsbury to Powis Castle, the early home of the Duchess of Northumberland. Hence the journey was made by Wynnstay, over the Menai Bridge, to the "Bulkeley Arms" at Beaumaris, which had been taken for a month. At the National Eisteddfod held here the Princess delighted the winners by presenting to them the prizes gained in the various competitions. An outbreak of cholera curtailed the stay at Beaumaris, whence the Duchess with her daughter moved to Plas

Newydd, which had been kindly placed at their disposal by the Marquess of Anglesey. The fine air and abundance of exercise had a most beneficial effect upon the Princess' constitution.

While staying at Plas Newydd, the Princess, on Saturday, October 13th, laid the first stone of the boys' school. On the 15th the royal party left Plas Newydd, and the Princess notes in her diary: "I looked out of the carriage window, that I might get a last look at the dear Emerald and her excellent crew." On the route to Eaton Hall, Bangor and Conway were passed, and at Kenmel Park, the seat of Lord Dinorben, the royal party stopped to meet the Duke of Sussex at luncheon. Passing through Holywell, they arrived at Eaton, escorted by the Yeomanry, under Lord Grosvenor. Escorts on the first part of the journey had been furnished by the Denbighshire and Flintshire Yeomanry. On the 17th of October a visit was made to Chester, where the visitors were received with much cheering by the great crowds which assembled from all the country round. The new bridge over the Dee was formallly opened, and received the name of "Victoria." From Eaton, again escorted by Lord Grosvenor and Lord Robert Grosvenor, at the head of their Yeomanry, the journey lay through Buxton to Chatsworth, where they were received by the Duke of Devonshire. On the next day the Princess Victoria planted an oak, and the Duchess of Kent a chestnut, near the terrace. Excursions were made to Haddon and to Hardwicke, also through Matlock to Belper, where Mr. Strutt's cotton mills were inspected with much interest. Leaving Chatsworth on the 24th, the party proceeded to Lord Lichfield's house at Shugborough, lunching on the way at Alton Towers, the magnificent

seat of Lord Shrewsbury. Here the Staffordshire Yeomanry was reviewed in the park. Next day Lichfield
Cathedral was visited, and addresses received from
the Mayor and Corporation. Passing through Stafford,
which was gaily decorated with arches and flowers, the
Duchess and the Princess, escorted by the Staffordshire
Yeomanry, arrived at Pitchford, where they were to be
the guests of Lord Liverpool. On one day during their
visit there was a meet of the hounds, who ran into their
fox under the carriage in which their Royal Highnesses
were sitting; on another day Shrewsbury and its old
school were visited.

Leaving Pitchford and passing through Church Stret-
ton, a stay was made at Oakley Court, the seat of Mr.
Clive. Thence the journey lay through Ludlow. Here
the mechanics formed a procession, Lord Clive and
Mr. Clive walking on foot at their head. At Tenbury
the Worcestershire Yeomanry relieved the Shropshire
Yeomanry as escort, and attended the carriage, Lord
Plymouth riding by the side, to Newell Grange, his
lordship's seat. During the two days which were passed
there, a visit was paid to Bromsgrove, where an address
was presented to the Duchess, and the Princess received
a present of a gold box full of small nails, as specimens
of the manufacture of the town.

The next day the homeward journey was continued
through Stratford-on-Avon, Shipstone-on-Stour, and
Woodstock, to Wytham Abbey, the seat of the Earl of
Abingdon. The Duchess and the Princess passed one
day in Oxford, where an address was presented by the
Vice-Chancellor of the University, Dr. Rowley, in the
Theatre, and another by the Mayor and Corporation in
the Town Hall; they were then escorted by Dean Gais-

ford through Christ Church, the Cathedral, and Library, and on to the Bodleian, where among other curiosities Princess Victoria took great interest in Queen Elizabeth's Latin exercise book, which she used when thirteen years old, the Princess' own age. The royal visitors were entertained at luncheon by the Vice-Chancellor at his own College, University, and after visiting New College were conducted to the University Press, with which the Princess was greatly pleased; here a copy of the Bible was presented to her, with a memorial of her visit printed on white satin. On the following day, the 9th of November, the journey was resumed through High Wycombe and Uxbridge to Kensington Palace. It is noted in the Princess' diary of the time, from which these particulars are taken by permission, that at all these visits the Princess dined at about seven o'clock with the Duchess of Kent and the guests.

Soon after their return home an interesting interview took place with Captain Back, who was preparing to start early in the following year, on his chivalrous enterprise to the Polar regions in search of Captain Ross. The Princess took extreme interest in the proposed route, which was explained by maps, and expressed much anxiety for the success of the expedition, and this interest in Polar exploration and its dangers has ever since been maintained.

The early part of the year 1833 was passed at Kensington. There the course of study was kept up as before, but the Princess now went out more in society and was seen more in public; twice during January she sat for her picture—to Wilkin and to Hayter. On the 25th of February, the birthday of Queen Adelaide, the Duchess of Kent and the Princess Victoria went to the

Qneen's Drawing Room. On this occasion they were
attended by the Duchess of Northumberland, Lady
Charlotte St. Maur, Lady Catherine Jenkinson, Lady
Cust, Sir John and Lady Conroy, Baroness Lehzen, Sir
Frederick Weterall and Sir George Anson. On Easter
Sunday their Royal Highness went as usual to the Chapel Royal at St. James'; on other days services was attended at Kensington Palace. On the 24th of April the
Duchess of Kent gave a dinner to the King; the Queen
was not well enough to be present. The Dukes of Cumberland and Gloucester were among the guests, who
numbered about thirty. Princess Victoria, on this as on
other similar occasions, did not dine, but went into the
drawing-room before dinner, and again after dinner till
the guests left.

On the 24th of May, the Princess' fourteenth birthday, she received a large number of presents, and in the
evening with the Duchess of Kent, and attended by the
Duchess of Northumberland and other members of her
suite, went to a juvenile ball given at St. James' Palace
by the King and Queen in honor of the day. The King
led her Royal Highness into the ballroom, and again to
supper, when the Princess sat between the King and
Qneen and her health was drunk by the company. On
the 28th the Princess again attended the Queen's Drawing Room, and records the impression made upon her by
the beauty of Lady Seymour, Mrs. Norton, Lady Clanri-
carde and others. In June the Duchess and Princess,
with the Princes Alexander and Ernest of Wurtemberg
and Prince Leiningen (all three staying on a visit at Kensington Palace), attended by the Duchess of Northumberland and others, drove to Woolwich, where they
visited the Arsenal, Barracks, and Storehouse, where

was preserved the carriage which had conveyed Napoleon to his tomb. They witnessed also the firing of several pieces of artillery.

At home the Princess' amusements were her pets, and her walks and drives, and during the Spring and Summer she much enjoyed riding. Another great enjoyment was the frequency of her visits to the opera, where she greatly enjoyed the performances of Duvernay and Taglioni, and listened with delight to Pasta, Malibran, Grisi, Tamburini, Rubini, and other celebrated singers, as well as to Paganini's playing on the violin.

During the Summer visits she paid both to Sion and Claremont, and on the 1st of July the Duchess of Kent and the Princess Victoria, accompanied by the Princes of Wurtemberg and Prince Leiningen and attended by Sir John and Lady Conroy and Baroness Lehzen, left Kensington en route for the Isle of Wight, passing by Esher, Guildford, and Petersfield to Portsmouth. The streets of the town were lined with troops, and Sir Colin Campbell rode beside the royal carriage. The Admiral, Sir Thomas Williams, took the royal party in his barge to the yacht Emerald, which was then towed by a steamer to Cowes, whence the party proceeded to Norris Castle, which was to be for the second time their abode. Sir John Conroy with his family lived at Osborne Lodge, an old thatched cottage which afterwards came into the possession of the Queen and stood on the present site of Osborne Cottage. From Norris Castle the Duchess with the Princess made many excursions to Southampton, Ryde, and the back of the Island; they attended divine service at the chuch at Whippingham, and were present at the consecration of the new church at East Cowes. On the 18th of July they went on board the

Emerald and were towed by the Messenger steamboat to Portsmouth. Here in the Admiral's barge they visited his flagship the Victory, and saw the spot on the deck where Nelson fell and the cockpit where he died. "The whole ship," notes Princess Victoria, "is remarkable for its neatness and order." A contemporary account states that the Duchess and the Princess tasted some of the men's dinner at one of their mess-tables, and much liked the fare.

On the 29th the Messenger again took the Emerald in tow for Weymouth, where the night was passed on shore at the Hotel. Addresses were presented and the town was illuminated in honor of the royal visitors, who next day left by road, escorted by the Dorsetshire Yeomanry, for Melbury, the seat of Lord Ilchester, where a stay was made of two nights; leaving again by the road, and, passing Beaminister and Bridport, they embarked on board the Emerald at Lyme Regis for Torquay, where they slept. During this journey the Duchess and Princess always slept on shore, as the accommodation on board was very scanty. On the afternoon of the 2nd, as the yacht was approaching Plymouth, the Admiral, Sir William Hargood, who had served under Nelson, and under the King, came on board. When entering the harbor, the little Emerald ran foul of the Active hulk, and those on board were in considerable danger. The mast was broken in two places by the collision, but did not fall, though many stories were current at the time of falling spars and rigging. No one was hurt, though every one was greatly frightened. The repair of the mast caused a delay of a couple of days. On the 3rd an address was presented by the Mayor and Corporation of Plymouth, and afterward Their Royal Highnesses and suite were present at a review of the 89th, 22nd, and 84th Regiments. The Duchess of Kent made a speech, in which she referred to her residence in the Isle of Wight, which enabled her, in pursuance of her system of education for her daughter, to visit the great ports and arsenals so intimately associated with the naval power and glories of the country. The Princess Victoria then presented new colors to the 89th Regiment, giving them into the hands of Ensigns Miles and Egerton. After the troops had marched past, and luncheon had been served at the Admiral's house, a visit was paid to the San Josef, the flagship, which had been taken by Nelson from the Spaniards at St. Vincent, a fine vessel of 120 guns, after which the Caledonia, 120 and the Revenge, 74, were inspected. On Sunday the Duchess and Princess attended morning services in the Dockyard Chapel, and in the afternoon rowed across to Mount Edgecumbe. Next day, on board the Forte frigate, Commander Pell, they sailed to the Eddystone Lighthouse. After lunch on board the sailors danced a hornpipe, and the royal party danced a quadrille and a country dance. The Princess danced first with Lieutenant Baker, and afterward with Captain Thiringham. They afterward landed on the Breakwater, whence they rowed to Mount Wise, and drove home. On Tuesday, the 6th, they re-embarked on the Emerald, the repairs to which had been completed, and, accompanied as far as the Sound by the Admiral and his captains, were again towed as far as Dartmouth, where they landede and drove to Torquay in the carriage of Mrs. Seale, as there were no post-horses to be had. They were expected to arrive by sea, and the change of plan caused some disappointment; however, a procession was formed of young girls with flowers, a little girl in the middle, the daughter of a sailor named Pepperill, carrying a crown. Leaving Torquay early next morning, and passing through Teignmouth and Dawlish, Exeter was reached, where the usual addresses were presented; thence through Honiton, Axminster, Bridport, Dorchester, and Wareham, Swanage was at last reached after a journey of 105 miles in thirteen and a half hours. Next morning the ladies of Swanage presented Princess Victoria with a straw bonnet, "the growth, make, and trade of the place," and later in the day, after returning on board the Emerald, the Duchess and Princess returned to Norris.

In the early part of the year 1834 there was less gaiety. The principal State ceremony of the year was when in June the Princess went with the King and Queen and Duchess of Kent to the first performance of the Royal Musical Festival at Westminster Abbey. The performance began with Handel's Coronation Anthem, and lasted for more than three hours. The Princess was everywhere greated with enthusiasm. Later, a house was taken at Tunbridge Wells for two months, and while there visits were paid to Lord Delaware at Buckhurst, and to Lord Camden at Bayham Abbey. Afterward a move was made to St. Leonards-on-Sea, where two very enjoyable months were passed.

The early part of 1835 was spent as usual at Kensington Palace. This year the Princess was present for the first time at Ascot Races, where she accompanied the King and Qneen in the State Procession. A description of the scene has been given by Mr. N. P. Willis: "In one of the intervals I walked under the King's Stand and I saw Her Majesty the Queen and the young Princess Victoria very distinctly. They were leaning over a railing listening to a ballad singer, and seeming as much interested and amused as any simple country folk could be. . . . The Princess is much better looking than any picture of her in the shops, and for the heir to such a crown as that of England, unnecessarily pretty and interesting. She will be sold, poor thing! bartered away by those dealers in Royal hearts, whose grand calculations will not be much consolation to her if she happens to have a taste of her own." The American did not turn out a true prophet.

On the 30th of July, 1835, the Princess having completed her sixteenth year, the ceremony of Confirmation was performed at the Chapel Royal, St. James', by the Archbishop of Canterbury, assisted by the Bishop of London, in the presence of the King and Queen and several members of the Royal Family. The scene is described as very touching, and the Princess, after the address of the Archbishop was profoundly affected. On the following Sunday, Divine Service was performed in the Chapel at Kensington Palace, and then the Princess, accompanied by her mother, received for the first time the Holy Sacrament from the hands of the Archbishop of Canterbury and the Dean of Chester, her preceptor. Soon after this a visit of a month was paid to Avoyne House, Tunbridge Wells, where, as also later in the year at Ramsgate, the Princess took much interest in the schools and the children educated in them. In September of this year another lengthy tour was made by Hatfield, Stamford, Grantham, Newark and Doncaster, to York, where their Royal Highnesses were for a week the guests of the Archbishop, Dr. Harcourt, at Bishopsthorpe, whence many visits were paid to the Minster. Leaving the Palace, a stay of three days was made with

Lord Harewood, when the journey was continued by Leeds, Wakefield and Barnsley, to Wentworth House, the seat of Lord Fitz-William. Here it was noticed that in the servants' hall the old style was retained and trenchers were still used. Rotherham and Newark were passed on the way to Belvoir Castle, where the Royal Party were entertained by the Duke of Rutland for some days. From Belvoir they passed to Burghley; here they remained for two nights, on the second of which a grand ball was given in their honor by their host, the Marquess of Exeter. Greville in his Memoirs says of it: "Three hundred people at the ball, which was opened by Lord Exeter and the Princess, who, after dancing one dance, went to bed."

They started early next morning by way of Peterborough, Thorney, Wisbeach, and King's Lynn, to Holkham, where they were the guests of the Earl of Leicester. Lord Albermarle, who was there to meet them, mentions that they were late for dinner in consequence of the enthusiastic loyalty of the people at Lynn, who insisted on drawing the carriage through the town. He also notes of the Royal visitors, "Both were affable. The youthful Princess in particular showed in her demeanor that winning courtesy with which millions of her subjects have since become familiar." Euston Hall, the seat of the Duke of Grafton, was the next house where a stay was made, from which the homeward journey was made without further interruption. Later, as has been mentioned, Ramsgate was visited, and a stay of a month there enabled the Princess to see Walmer Castle and Dover.

The event of most importance in the following year was the arrival at Kensington Palace, on a visit of some

weeks, of the Duke of Coburg with his two sons Ernest
and Albert. Then, for the first time, the Queen saw her
future husband. The visit was brought about by the
agency of King Leopold, who in this carired out the
long-cherished idea of his mother, the Dowager Duchess
of Coburg, who had early set her heart on the union of
her two grandchildren. They were received with every
attention by the King and Queen, and the other members
of the Royal family, and spent a busy time in seeing all
they could in London and the neighborhood. They
were much impressed by the sight of the great anniversary gathering of the children of the charity schools in
Saint Paul's, after which they enjoyed the hospitality of
the Lord Mayor at the Mansion House. Of this visit
Prince Albert writes on the 1st of June, 1836: "My first
appearance was a levee of the King's, which was long
and fatiguing but very interesting. The same evening
we dined at Court, and at night there was a beautiful
concert, at which we had to stand till two o'clock. The
next day the King's birthday was kept. We went in
the middle of the day to a drawing-room at St. James'
Palace, at which about 3,800 people passed before the
King and Queen and the other high dignitaries to offer
their congratulations. There was again a great dinner in
the evening and then a concert which lasted till one
o'clock. You can well imagine that I had many hard
battles to fight against sleepiness during these late entertainments. The day before yesterday, Monday, our
Aunt gave a brilliant ball here at Kensington Palace, at
which the gentlemen appeared in uniform and the
ladies in so-called fancy dresses. We remained till four
o'clock. Duke William of Brunswick, the Prince of Orange and his two sons, and the Duke of Wellington, were

the only guests that you will care to hear about. Yesterday we spent with the Duke of Northumberland at Sion, and now we are going to Claremont. From this account you will see how constantly engaged we are, and that we must make the most of our time to see at least some of the sights in London. Dear Aunt is very kind to us, and does everything she can to please us, and our Cousin also is very amiable." Almost simultaneously with the departure of the Prince from England, King Leopold spoke to his niece on the subject of his wishes, and in writing to him on the 7th of June the Princess concludes her letter by saying: "I have now only to beg you, my dearest Uncle, to take care of the health of one now so dear to me, and to take him under your special protection. I hope and trust that all will go on prosperously and well on this subject now of so much importance to me."

The Autumn of this year, after a visit to Lord Liverpool at Buxted Park, near Uckfield, was spent quietly at Ramsgate.

On the 24th of May, 1837, the Princess attained her majority; she was wakened by a serenade, and later received a number of costly presents, including a grand piano from the King, who earnestly wished to see his niece of age before his death. The day was kept a general holiday at Kensington, there were addresses of congratulation from many public bodies, among them one from the Corporation of London, to which the Duchess of Kent replied: ". . . The Princess has arrived at that age, which now justifies my expressing my confident expectation, that she will be found competent to execute the sacred trust which may be reposed in her; for, communicating as she does with all classes of society, she cannot but perceive that the greater the diffusion of religious knowledge and the love of freedom in a country, the more orderly, industrious and wealthy is its population; and that with the desire to preserve the constitutional prerogatives of the Crown ought to be co-ordinate the protection of the liberty of the people." To the address presented to herself the Princess simply replied: "I am very thankful for your kindness, and my mother has expressed all my feelings." On the evening of this day a State ball was given at St. James', at which neither the King nor Queen were able to be present, both being very ill. The Princess opened the ball with Lord Fitzalan, the eldest son of the Duke of Norfolk, and danced also with Prince Esterhazy. Before her next appearance at St. James' the Princess had succeeded to the throne.

Many portraits were painted during her early years, of the Princess upon whom the hopes of the nation were fixed. One of the earliest is given at the head of this chapter; it is from a miniature painted by Anthony Stewart, who had come from Scotland to London, where he painted a miniature of Princess Charlotte, which brought him to the notice of Prince Leopold. He was one of the first to paint a miniature of the Princess, who afterwards sat to him repeatedly, and the engraving from these very delicate works were exceedingly popular. Shortly afterwards the Duchess of Kent sat with her daughter to Sir William Beechey, whose portraits of the Royal Family are well known; in this picture, of which a reproduction is given, the infant Princess stands on the sofa where her mother is sitting, and holds in her hand a miniature of her father. This picture was painted especially for Prince Leopold. Another charming portrait of the Princess is that by Westall, in which she is represented as sketching from nature. Westall, as has been mentioned before, was drawing-master for the Princess; he died in 1836, so that this picture is probably one of his latest works. In 1833 it has been noted above that the Princess sat for her portrait to Wilkin and to Hayter. Of the work of the latter a reproduction is given. The Princess stands at a table holding a rose in her right hand, and from her left hangs a light scarf; the glove from her right hand is the plaything of her favorite dog; in the background is seen the newly-raised Round Tower of Windsor Castle. The portrait by Wilkin taken at the same time only exists in a somewhat rare lithograph; in it the hair is plaited on the crown in the same manner as in Hayter's picture. Of other early portraits mention may be made of a bust by Behnes, taken when the Princess was very young. It is now in the corridor at Windsor Castle, and is widely known by an engraving which had extensive circulation at the time, but gives a most distorted view of the excellent original. The portrait of the Duchess of Kent introduced in this chapter is taken from a miniature painting by Collen, after a picture painted in 1835 by Sir George Hayter; in it may be traced the great likeness borne by the Duchess to her brother King Leopold, and also to her mother.

CHAPTER FOUR.

The demise of the Crown by the death of King William IV. had been expected for some time. On Tuesday, the 20th of June, 1837, at twelve minutes past two, His Majesty expired. The Archbishop of Canterbury, who had performed the last religious rites, and Lord Conyngham, Lord Chamberlain, who was also in attendance, started as soon as was possible from Windsor, to convey the news to Kensington. They arrived at five in the morning, and with some difficulty aroused the sleeping household. After much delay, an attendant stated that the Princess was in such a sweet sleep that she could not be disturbed; to which the messenger replied: "We have come on business of State to the Queen, and even her sleep must give way to that." In a few minutes she came into the room, a shawl thrown over her dressing-gown, her feet in slippers, and her hair falling down her back. She had been wakened by the Duchess of Kent, who told Her Majesty she must get up; she went alone into the room where Lord Conyngham and the Archbishop were waiting. The Lord Chamberlain then knelt down, and presenting a paper announcing the death of her uncle to the Queen; and the Archbishop said he had come by desire of Queen Adelaide, who thought the Queen would like to hear in what a peaceful state the

King had been at the last. Meanwhile, at the Council
Office, to which the news of the late King's death had
been conveyed by special messenger from Windsor, sum-
monses were issued with all possible haste to the Privy
Counsellors to atend at Kensington, to present a loyal
address of fealty, and to offer homage. This address,
which had been kept in readiness, was conveyed at once
to the Palace by Mr. Barrett Lennard, chief clerk of the
Council Office, whose son, acting as his private secretary,
has comunicated an account of the ceremony, of which he
is now, besides Her Majesty, the only survivor. In the
antechamber to which they were introduced six persons
at most were present, among whom were the Duke of
Sussex and the Duke of Wellington, with Lord Melbourne, who had previously been received in audience
alone at 9 a. m.

Subsequently about a dozen ministers, prelates and
Officials, were admitted when the doors were closed.
The address was real aloud and signed by the Duke of
Sussex and then by the others present, after which the
doors were opened, "disclosing a large State Saloon,
close to whose threshold there stood unattended a small,
slight, fair-complexioned young lady apparently fifteen
years of age. She was attired in a close-fitting dress of
black silk, her light hair parted and drawn from her
forehead; she wore no ornament whatever on her dress
or person. The Duke of Sussex advanced, embraced, and
kissed her—his niece, the Queen. Lord Melbourne and
others kissed hands in the usual form, and the usher
taking the address, closed the folding doors, and the
Queen disappeared from our gaze. No word was uttered by Her Majesty or by any present, and no sound
broke the silence, which seemed to me to add to the im-

pressive solemnity and interest of the scence." The subsequent meeting of the Queen's first Council has been described by many of those who were privileged to attend it; and a fairly accurate picture of it has been painted by Sir David Wilkie, who, at the expense of truth, has emphasized the principal figure by painting her in a white dress instead of the black which was actually worn, the Queen being already in mourning for the death of the mother of Queen Adelaide. The Council met at eleven o'clock, and at that hour the Queen, who had been accompanied to the adjoining room by her mother, was met by her uncles, the Dukes of Cumberland and Sussex, who introduced her to the Council Chamber, where she took her seat on a chair at the head of the table. No better description of the scene can be given than that, often quoted, by Greville, clerk of the Council: "Never was anything like the first impression she produced, or the chorus of praise and admiration which is raised about her manner and behavior, and certainly not without justice. It was very extraordinary, and something far beyond what was looked for. Her extreme youth and inexperience, and the ignorance of the world concerning her, naturally excited intense curiosity to see how she would act on this trying occasion, and there was a considerable assemblage at the palace, notwithstanding the short notice which was given.
* * * She bowed to the Lords, took her seat, and then read her speech in a clear, distinct, and audible voice, and without any appearance of fear or embarrassment. She was quite plainly dressed and in mourning.

"After she had read her speech, and taken and signed the oath for the security of the Church of Scotland, the Privy Counsellors were sworn, the two Royal Dukes (of Cumberland and Sussex) first, by themselves; and as these two old men, her uncles, knelt before her, swearing allegiance and kissing her hand, I saw her blush up to the eyes, as if she felt the contrast between their civil and their natural relations, and this was the only sign of emotion which she evinced. Her manner to them was very graceful and engaging; she kissed them both, and rose from her chair and moved towards the Duke of Sussex, who was farthest from her and too infirm to reach her. She seemed rather bewildered at the multitude of men who were sworn, and who came one after another to kiss her hand, but she did not speak to anybody, nor did she make the slightest difference in her manner, or show any in her countenance, to any individual of any rank, station, or party. I particularly watched her when Melbourne and the Ministers and the Duke of Wellington and Peel approached her. She went through the whole ceremony—occasionally looking at Melbourne for instruction when she had any doubt what to do, which hardly ever occurred—with perfect calmness and self-possession, but at the same time with a graceful modesty and propriety particularly interesting and ingratiating. When the business was done she retired as she had entered. * * * Peel said how amazed he was at her manner and behavior, at her apparent deep sense of her situation, her modesty, and at the same time her firmness. She appeared, in fact, to be awed. but not daunted, and afterwards the Duke of Wellington told me the same thing, and added that if she had been his own daughter he could not have desired to see her perform her part better." This description from the pen of one not given to flattery, is corroborated by the testimony of many others present.

Earl Grey writes to the Princess Lieven:—"When called upon for the first time to appear before the Privy Council, and to take upon herself the awful duties with which at so early an age she has been so suddenly charged, there was in her appearance and demeanor a composure, a propriety, an aplomb, which were quite extraordinary. She never was in the least degree confused, embarrassed, or hurried; read the declaration beautifully; went through the forms of business as if she had been accustomed to them all her life." Lord Palmerston says in a letter to Lord Granville:— "The Queen went through her task with great dignity and self-possession; one saw she felt much inward emotion, but it was fully controlled. Her articulation was particularly good, her voice remarkably pleasing."

The same impression was conveyed by her demeanor at her High Council on the day following, at St. James's; here, at 10 o'clock, the new monarch was formally proclaimed Queen of Great Britain and Ireland. The quadrangle of the palace in front of the window where Her Majesty was to appear was filled by her loyal subjects, conspicuous among whom was Daniel O'Connell, waving his hat and cheering vociferously. A salute was fired in St. James's Park, and the Queen appeared at the window of the Presence Chamber, beneath which were posted the heralds, headed by the Duke of Norfolk, Earl Marshal of England, and Sir William Woods (father of the present Garter King-at-Arms), the Sergeants-at-Arms, and State trumpeters. Sir William Woods, acting Garter King-at-Arms, read the Proclamation announcing the Queen's accession, and ending with the words "to whom we do acknowledge all faith and constant obedience, with all hearty ad humble affection, beseeching God, by whom all Kings and Queens do reign, to bless the royal Princess Victoria with long and happy years to reign over us. God save the Queen." The band of the Guards then played the National Anthem amid the cheers of the crowd.

The second Council was held at noon, of which Greville writes: "She presided with as much ease as if she had been doing nothing else all her life, and though Lord Lansdowne and my colleague had contrived between them to make some confusion with the Council papers, she was not put out by it. She looked very well, and though so small in stature, and without much pretension to beauty, the gracefulness of her manner and the good expression of her countenance, give her on the whole a very agreeable appearance, and with her youth inspire an excessive interest in all who approach her, and which I can't help feeling myself. After the Council she received the Archbishops and Bishops, and after them the Judges." Crabb Robinson, in his diary, relates an incident which proves that, though the Queen could behave with extraordinary dignity when it was required, she had not lost the gaiety and spirit of her youth. "The Bishop of London told Amyot," he says, "that when the Bishops were first presented to the Queen, she received them with all possible dignity and then retired. She passed through a glass door, and, forgetting its transparency, was seen to run off like a girl as she is. * * * This is just as it should be. If she had not now the high spirits of a girl of eighteen, we should have less reason to hope she would turn out a sensible woman at thirty."

On the morning of her accession one of the first acts of the new Queen was to write a letter of condolence to

her widowed Aunt Adelaide, now Queen Dowager. This
she addressed to "Her Majesty, the Queen;" it was
pointed out that the correct address would have the additional word "Dowager," but she refused to make the
alteration, saying, "I will not be the first person to re-
mind her of it." Greville remarks of this, "Conyngham,
when he came to her with the intelligence of the King's
death, brought a request from the Queen Dowager that
she might be permitted to remain at Windsor till after
the funeral, and she has written a letter couched in the
kindest terms, begging her to consult nothing but her
own health and convenience, and to remain at Windsor
just as long as she pleases. In short, she appears to
act with every sort of good taste and good feeling, as
well as good sense, and as far as it has gone nothing can
be more favorable than the impression she has made,
and nothing can promise better than her manner and
conduct. * * * The young Queen, who might well
be either dazzled or confounded with the grandeur and
novelty of her situation, seems neither the one nor the
other, and behaves with a propriety and decorum beyond her years."

Of all the letters and congratulations received at this
time by the Queen, we may well believe that the most
welcome was that from her cousin, Prince Albert, who,
on hearing of the late King's death, wrote instantly as
follows:—

"BONN, 26th June, 1837.

"MY DEAREST COUSIN:—I must write you a few
lines to present you my sincerest felicitations on that
great change which has taken place in your life. Now
you are the Queen of the mightiest land of Europe, in
your hand lies the happiness of millions. May Heaven

assist you and strengthen you with its strength in that
high and difficult task. I hope that your reign may be
long, happy, and glorious, and that your efforts may be
rewarded by the thankfulness and love of your subjects.
May I pray you to think, likewise, sometimes of your
cousins in Bonn, and to continue to them that kindness you favored them with till now. Be assured that
our minds are always with you. I will not be indiscreet
and abuse your time. Believe me, always, your Majesty's most obedient and faithful servant,

"ALBERT."

This is the first letter written by the Prince in English,
and shows what proficiency he had made in the language so soon to be his own. "How much," says one
who had deeply studied his character, "of the Prince's
great nature is visible in it—though addressed to a
young and powerful Queen; there is not a word of flattery in it. His first thought is of the great responsibility
of the position, the happiness of the millions that was
at stake. Then comes the anxious hope that the reign
may be glorious, and then how gracefully and naturally
the tender regard of an affectionate relation comes in
at the last." To his father, at the same time, he writes,
"The death of the King of England has everywhere
caused the greatest sensation. From what Uncle Leopold, as well as Aunt, writes to us, the new reign has
begun most successfully. Cousin Victoria is said to have
shown astonishing self-possession. She undertakes a
heavy responsibility, especially at the present moment,
when parties are so excited, and all rest their hopes on
her. Poor Aunt has again been violently attacked in

the newspapers, but she has also found strenuous sup-
porters."

On the 13th of July, the Queen and the Duchess of
Kent, greatly to the regret of the loyal subjects of the
royal suburb, took their departure from Kensington to
take up their residence at Buckingham Palace, formerly
known as the Queen's House, having been bought by
George III., and settled on Queen Charlotte, in lieu of
Somerset House, the ancient home of the Queens of
England. It was rebuilt by George IV., but not completed till the reign of William IV., who disliked it extremely, and never lived there. The Queen was greeted
with hearty cheers, and seemed to leave with much regret
the place of her birth and the home of her childhood.
From Buckingham Palace four days later, she went in
state to dissolve Parliament; the route from the Palace
to the House of Parliament was densely thronged to see
the young Queen, who was dressed, on this occasion,
in white, with a tiara of brilliants, and wore the ribbon
of the Garter over her shoulder. At three o'clock she
entered the House of Lords, and ascended the throne;
when, prompted by Lord Melbourne, who stood by her
side, she desired the Lords to be seated. Her Majesty
then read her speech, with that clear intonation for which
her voice has always been distinguished, concluding by
saying: "I ascend the throne with a deep sense of the
responsibility which is imposed upon me; but I am supported by the consciousness of my right intentions, and
by my dependence upon the protection of Almighty God.
It will be my care to strengthen our institutions, civil
and ecclesiastical, by discreet improvement, wherever
improvement is required ;and to to do all in my power
to compose and allay animosity and discord.   Acting

upon these principles, I shall, upon all occasions, look with confidence to the wisdom of Parliament and the affections of my people, which form the true support of the dignity of the Crown, and ensure the stability of the Constitution." Among those present in the House of Lords was Fanny Kemble, than whom no one could have been more competent to give an opinion on elocution: "The enunciation was as perfect as the intonation was melodious, and I think it is impossible to hear a more excellent utterance than that of the Queen's English by the English Queen." The American statesman, Charles Sumner, was also present, and has recorded his own impression: "Her voice is sweet and finely modulated, and she pronounced every word distinctly and with a just regard to its meaning; I think I never heard anything better read in my life than her speech."

On the 22d of the following month the Queen removed with the Court to Windsor Castle, where she soon had the pleasure of welcoming her uncle, King Leopold, and his consort, Queen Louise. Of this first sojourn at Windsor some interesting details are preserved in the diary of the late Sir Charles Murray, who was then a newly appointed Groom-in-Waiting, from which post he was shortly afterwards promoted to be Master of the Household. On his arrival at Windsor, he writes: "I was presented and kissed hands, after which I joined the cavalcade, consisting of twenty-five or thirty equestrians, and we made a promenade about the Great Park for two hours. There was little or no form or ceremony observed as to precedence. The Queen rode generally in front, accompanied by the Queen of the Belgians (who was here on a short visit with her royal husband), and the King, the Duchess of

Kent, and now and then she called up Lords Conyngham, Wellington, or Melbourne to ride beside her. Her
Majesty's seat on horseback is easy and graceful, and
the early habit of command observable in all her movements and gestures, is agreeably relieved by the gentle
tone of voice, and the natural playfulness, with which
she addresses her relatives or the ladies about her. I
never saw a more quick or observant eye. In the course
of the ride it glanced occasionally over every individual
of the party, and I am sure that neither absence nor im-
propriety of any kind could escape detection. At half-
past seven the guests and the household again met Her
Majesty in the corridor, and we proceeded to dinner,
the arrangements for which were handsome and without parade. The ladies retired to the drawing room, and
we followed in a quarter of an hour. The band was in
attendance at and after dinner, and played some excellent music, chiefly of Rossini and Bellini. During the
evening Her Majesty conversed with her principal
guests. She also played two games at draughts with
the Queen of the Belgians, both of which she gained.
Quod felix faustumque omen. There was a whist table,
consisting of the Duchess of Kent, the King of the Belgians, Duke of Wellington, and Lilford."

A few days after he writes: "We rode out at four, and
as the King and Queen of the Belgians were of the party,
we went rather slow and had but a short ride. * * *
Our young Queen's manner to King Leopold is most
respectful and affectionate; indeed, her manner to every-
one about her is perfectly winning and appropriate, and
her countenance lights up with the most agreeable and
intelligent expression possible. September 10th.—This
being Sunday we accompanied Her Majesty to the

Chapel, and the party included her royal visitors, as well as the Chancellor, the Premier, Master of the Horse, etc. In the afternoon she took a short drive in the Great Park, and I went out on the terrace, which presented a very gay and beautiful appearance, as the bands both of the Grenadiers and Life Guards were playing near the new fountain, and all the officers of the two regiments, as well as the belles of Windsor and the neighborhood, were enjoying their holiday promenade. At dinner I had a very interesting conversation with Baroness Lehzen, who has been for many years Her Majesty's governess and preceptress. I know of nothing more creditable to herself or to her illustrious pupil, than the fact that one of the first acts of her reign was to secure and retain her preceptress in an honorable situation about her own person. Her Majesty treats the Baroness with the most kind and affectionate confidence, and the latter tells me that she has carefully copied every letter of private correspondence of her young mistress, both before and since her coming to the throne; but that, since she has been Queen, Her Majesty has never shown her one letter of Cabinet or State documents, nor has she spoken to her, nor to any woman about her, upon party or political questions. As Queen she reserves all her confidence for her official advisers, while, as a woman, she is frank, gay, and unreserved as when she was a young girl. What a singular and excellent judgment is shown in this—Heaven grant it may be kept up, and rewarded by the affection and prosperity of her subjects. I had a long conversation with her on the 24th, while riding, chiefly on the subject of modern languages. She speaks French perfectly, and both reads and understands German, but does not like speaking it. Her Majesty is also a good Italian scholar. Her conversation is very agreeable; both her ideas and language are natural and original, while there is a latent independence of mind and strength of judgment discernible through the feminine gentleness of tone in which her voice is pitched. Every day that I have passed here has increased my admiration of the excellent judgment shown by Mme. de Lehzen in her education, and of the amiable and grateful feeling evinced by Her Majesty towards her governess. It does the highest honor to both. There is another person in the household whose character it is not easy to penetrate, or to describe, Baron Stockmar. He is certainly possessed of great abilities, but is silent and reserved, while his general state of health seems almost to preclude the possibility of his being lively or communicative. At dinner he eats nothing, and talks less than he eats; but I observe that he holds quiet conversations with Lords Melbourne and Palmerston in the morning, and I should think it likely that he was much in the confidence of the Queen. He is a most intimate and faithful friend of the King of the Belgians. A day or two ago, she (the Queen) inspected the Life Guards and Grenadiers, on horseback, accompanied by the Duchess of Kent, Lord Hill, Conyngham, and the rest of her suite. She was dressed in a habit of the Windsor uniform, and wore a military cap, with a gold band passing under the chin. As the several companies and squadrons passed and saluted her, she raised her hand and returned the salute of each; and the grave earnestness of her manner as well as the graceful self-possession of her attitude struck me particularly."

These graphic details give a pleasing impression of the routine of the Court life, and, indeed, with a few alterations, a tolerably accurate description of the manner in which the time is passed at the present day. Here, also, is recorded the first impression made on a shrewd observer by that remarkable man who afterwards so unobtrusively, but so powerfully, influenced the conduct of affairs in the British Court, by his profound knowledge and practical wisdom.

In the autumn of the year 1837 the Court moved to Brighton, but the stay at the Pavilion was not prolonged, as the crowding mob, whenever the gates of the grounds were passed, was anything but pleasant. Returning to London on the 4th of November, Her Majesty on the 9th paid her first visit, in state, to the City of London, and dined with the Lord Mayor in the Guildhall. The Queen traveled in the state carriage, attended by the Mistress of the Robes and the Master of the Horse, and escorted by the Life Guards, along the Strand to the Guildhall. At Temple Bar the procession halted, and the keys of the city were dutifully offered and graciously returned to the Lord Mayor, who then mounted his horse, and holding the City Sword, preceded the royal carriage. At St. Paul's another halt was made, and the Senior Scholar of Christ's Hospital, according to ancient custom, delivered an address of welcome. On this occasion the great City Hall was magnificently decorated, and plate of fabulous value was displayed. In return for this splendid entertainment Her Majesty conferred a baronetcy on the Lord Mayor, and was pleased to knight both the Sheriffs, one of whom was Mr. Moses Montefiore, the first of his faith to receive the honor from an English Sovereign. On the 24th of December, after going to the Houses of Parliament before the recess, the Queen went to Windsor for the Christmas holidays. At this session of Parliament the details of the Queen's civil list had been arranged and passed, the whole amounting to the sum of £385,000 per annum.

From the moment of her accession to the throne, she had been constantly brought into the most intimate relations with the Prime Minister, of whom Greville writes: "No man is more formed to ingratiate himself with her than Melbourne. He treats her with unbounded consideration and respect; he consults her taste and her wishes, and he puts her at her ease by his frank and natural manner, while he amuses her by the quaint, queer, epigramatic turn of his mind, and his varied knowledge upon all subjects. It is not, therefore, surprising that she should be well content with her present government, and that during the progress of the elections she should have testified great interest in the success of the Whig candidates. Her reliance upon Melbourne's advice extends at present to subjects quite beside his constitutional functions, for the other day somebody asked her permission to dedicate some novel to her, when she said she did not like to grant the permission without knowing the contents of the work, and she desired Melbourne to read the book, and let her know if it was fit that she should accept the dedication. Melbourne read the first volume, but found it so dull that he would not read any more, and sent her word that she had better refuse, which she accordingly did. She seems to be liberal, but at the same time prudent with regard to money, for when the Queen Dowager proposed to her to take her band into her service, she declined to incur so great an expense without further consideration, but one of the first things she spoke to Melbourne about was the payment of her father's debts, which she is resolved to discharge"—and they were discharged accordingly. Later he writes on the same subject: "George Villiers, who came from Windsor on Monday, told me he had been exceedingly struck with Lord Melbourne's manner to the Queen, and hers to him; his, so parental and anxious, but always so respectful and deferential; hers, indicative of such entire confidence, such pleasure in his society. She is constantly talking to him; let who will be there, he always sits next her at dinner, and evidently by arrangement, because he always takes in the lady-in-waiting, which necessarily places him next her, the etiquette being that the lady-in-waiting sits next but one to the Queen. It is not unnatural, and to him it is peculiarly interesting. I have no doubt he is passionately fond of her, as he might be of his own daughter if he had one, and the more because he is a man with a capacity for loving without having anything in the world to love. It is become his province to educate, instruct, and form the most interesting mind and character of the world. No occupation was ever more engrossing or involved greater responsibility. I have no doubt that Melbourne is both equal to and worthy of the task, and that it is fortunate that she has fallen into his hands, and that he discharges this great duty wisely, honorably, and conscientiously. There are, however, or rather may be hereafter, inconveniences in the establishment of such an intimacy, and in a connection of so close and affectionate a nature between the young Queen and her Minister; for whenever the Government, which hangs by a thread, shall be broken up, the parting will be painful, and their subsequent relations will not be without embarrassment to themselves, nor fail to be the cause of jealousy in others. It is a great proof of the discretion

and purity of his conduct and behavior that he is admired, respected, and liked by all the Court." This rupture, however, apparently so imminent, did not occur till
another, and a permanent counsellor, took his place as a
husband by the Queen's side.

On the 27th of June, 1838, the Queen was crowned in
Westminster Abbey, an event which, on account of the
age and sex of the Sovereign, excited an extraordinary
degree of interest among all classes. It was afterwards
computed that no less than four hundred thousand persons came into London to see the procession and festivities, and that upwards of £200,000 was in consequence
expended. The ceremonial was conducted in nearly all
respects in the same manner as that of the coronation
of William IV.; the walking procession of all the estates of the realm, the banquet in Westminster Hall, with
all the feudal services attendant thereon, being dispensed
with; not without some protests from the antiquaries, as
well as from interested tradesmen. The procession, however, outside the Abbey was considerably increased in
number as well as in splendor, and the route from the
Palace to the Abbey lengthened, so as to give the vast
throngs of people more opportunity of seeing their Sovereign. As nearly as possible at ten o'clock the Queen
stepped into her carriage, a new Royal Standard (30 by
18 feet), was hoisted on the Marble Arch, the bands
played the National Anthem, and a salute of twenty-one
guns was fired in the Park. Following the Trumpeters
and Life Guards came the magnificent State Carriages
of the Foreign Ambassadors, a novel sight on such an
occasion. Conspicuous among them was the splendid
coach of Marshal Soult, Duke of Dalmatia, the old an-
tagonist of the Duke of Wellington, and now Ambassa-

dor from the King of the French; the veteran was greeted all along the line of procession, and even in the Abbey itself, with the heartiest cheers. Next came the members of the Royal Family, preceding the Queen's carriages, conveying the Members and Officers of the Household; after which, surrounded by a brilliant staff and escort, came the State Carriage bearing the Sovereign, in attendance upon whom were the Mistress of the Robes, the Duchess of Sutherland, and the Master of the Horse, the Earl of Albemarle; the Captain-General of the Royal Archers, the Duke of Buccleuch, on horseback, followed the carriage.

The Queen reached the west door of the Abbey at half-past eleven, and was there received by the great Officers of State, the noblemen bearing the Regalia, and the Bishops carrying the Patina, the Chalice and the Bible. Her Majesty then repaired to her robing chamber, and soon after twelve the grand procession passed up the nave into the choir, in the centre of which was a raised dais covered with cloth of gold, on which was placed the chair of homage. Farther on, within the chancel and facing the altar, was placed St. Edward's chair. The altar was covered with magnificent gold plate. As the Queen advanced, the anthem, "I was glad when they said unto me, Let us go into the House of the Lord," was sung by the choir, at the close of which the boys of Westminster School shouted "Vivat Victoria Regina." Then, amid a solemn hush, the Queen passed to a faldstool and knelt in silent prayer, after which the ceremonial proceeded. First came "The Recognition," by the Archbishop of Canterbury, who advanced to the Queen, accompanied by the Lord Chancellor, the Lord Great Chamberlain, the Lord High Constable, and the

Earl Marshal, preceded by the Deputy-Garter, and repeated these words: "Sirs, I here present unto you Queen Victoria, the undoubted Queen of this realm; wherefore all you who are come this day to do your homage, are you willing to do the same?" In answer burst forth the universal cry, "God save Queen Victoria," repeated as the Archbishop turned to the north, south, and west, the Queen turning at the same time in the same direction. Her Majesty then advanced to the altar and made her first offering of a pall or altar cloth of gold, which was laid on the altar, on which had been previously placed the Chalice, Patina, and Bible. An ingot of gold, of one pound weight, was then presented by the Queen to the Archbishop, by whom it was placed in the oblation-basin. After the Litany and the first portion of the Communion Service, the Sermon was preached by the Bishop of London, at the conclusion of which the Oath was administered by the Archbishop of Canterbury. After asking the Queen if she would govern according to the Statutes of Parliament, and the laws and customs of the realm, and whether she would cause law and justice in mercy to be executed, he further asked: "Will you, to the uttermost of your power, maintain the laws of God, the true profession of the Gospel, and the Protestant reformed religion, established by law; and will you maintain and preserve inviolably, the settlement of the United Church of England and Ireland, and the doctrine, worship, discipline, and government thereof as by law established, within England and Ireland, and the territory thereunto belonging; and will you preserve unto the Bishops and Clergy of England and Ireland, and to the churches there committed to their charges, all such rights and privileges as by law do or shall appertain to them or any of them?" Having answered these questions in the affirmative, and preceded by the Great Officers of State, Her Majesty went to the altar, where kneeling, and with her right hand upon the Gospels held before her by the Archbishop, she said: "The things which I have here before promised I will perform and keep. So help me God." The Queen having kissed the book, and signed a transcript of the Oath, then knelt upon the faldstool while the choir sang, "Veni, Creator, Spiritus."

The Archbishop then said the prayer preceding the anointing, after which the choir sang the Coronation Anthem, at the beginning of which the Queen retired to St. Edward's Chapel with her ladies and train-bearers, and was divested of her crimson robe and kirtle. She then put on the super-tunica of cloth of gold, also in the shape of a kirtle, over a linen gown trimmed with lace, and taking off her circlet of diamonds returned bareheaded to the Abbey, where she took her seat in King Edward's chair; four Knights of the Garter held over her head a rich canopy of cloth of gold, the Archbishop then anointed the head and hands of the Sovereign, marking them in the form of a cross, and pronouncing the words, "Be thou anointed with holy oil, as kings, priests, and prophets were anointed. And as Solomon was anointed King by Zadok the priest and Nathan the prophet, so be you anointed, blessed and consecrated Queen over this people, whom the Lord your God hath given you to rule and govern, in the name of the Father and of the Son and of the Holy Ghost, Amen." A benediction from the Archbishop followed; after which the spurs were presented by the Lord Great Chamberlain, and the Sword of State by Lord Melbourne, who, according to custom, redeemed it with a hundred shillings, and carried it unsheathed during the rest of the ceremony.

The Queen, who had been invested with the Imperial mantle, or dalmatic robe of cloth of gold lined with ermine, then received the Orb, which she found very heavy. In the investure "per annulum et baculum," the ring and sceptre, which followed, it was found that the ring was too small, and it was only by great exertion that it could be placed on the third finger, where it caused great pain, and could only be removed after the ceremony by bathing the hand in iced water. The Archbishop having offered a prayer to God to bless Her Majesty and "crown her with all princely virtues," received the crown from the Dean, and reverently placed it on the Queen's head. This was no sooner done than from every part of the Abbey rose a loud and enthusiastic cry of "God save the Queen!" At this moment, the Peers and Peeresses present put on their coronets, the Bishops their caps, and the Kings-at-Arms their crowns; the trumpets sounded, the drums beat, and salutes were fired by signal from the Park and Tower guns. The Bible was then presented to the Queen. She returned it to the Archbishop, who, after restoring it to the altar, pronounced the Benediction, after which the "Te Deum" was sung by the choir, and the Queen was then "enthroned" or "lifted," according to the formulary, by the Archbishops, Bishops, and Peers surrounding her, into the chair of homage, where first the Archbishop of Canterbury knelt, and did homage for himself and other Lord Spirituals, who all kissed the Queen's hand. Then the Queen's uncles, the Dukes of Sussex and Cambridge, removing their coronets, did homage in these words:

"I do become your liegeman of life and limb, and of earthly worship; and faith and truth I will bear unto you, to live and die, against all manner of folks. So help me God." They touched the Crown on the Queen's head, kissed her left cheek, and retired; it was noticed that Her Majesty's bearing to her uncles was very affectionate. Then, according to their precedence, the Dukes and other Peers performed their homage, the senior of each rank reciting the words, each Peer kissing Her Majesty's hand and touching the Crown. The aged Lord Rolle, who was over eighty, trying to mount the steps, fell down, and with difficulty was raised. He again attempted to perform his duty, when the Queen, rising from her seat, went to meet him, to prevent him coming up farther, and extended her hand to him to kiss; "an act of graciousness and kindness which made a very great sensation."

While the homage was performed by the Lords, the Earl of Surrey, Lord Treasurer of the Household, threw to the occupants of the choir, and the lower galleries, the silver Coronation medals; these were scrambled for with great eagerness. After the homage was over, the Anthem, "This is the day which the Lord hath made," was sung, followed by the sound of the drums and trumpets, and nine loud and hearty cheers from the House of Commons, who then joined in the homage. The remainder of the Communion Service was then read, and the Queen, divested of the symbols of Sovereignty, received the Holy Sacrament; then resuming her crown, and holding the sceptre, she took her seat on the Throne, when the Service was concluded, and the final blessing pronounced, followed by the singing of the "Hallelujah Chorus." This ended the long ceremonial;

Her Majesty left the Throne, and proceeded to the west door of the Abbey, wearing the Crown, her right hand holding the Sceptre with the Cross, and the left supporting the Orb; she was followed by the Peers and Peeresses, now wearing their coronets, and the brilliant afternoon sun pouring through the windows made the scene one of incomparable splendor. Along the homeward route the manifestations of loyalty were even more enthusiastic than in the morning; for the Queen was now fully apparelled in State, and wore the Crown, in the front of which blazed the historic ruby of Poitiers and Agincourt. Mrs. Jamieson, who witnessed the procession, writes: "When she returned, looking pale and tremulous, crowned, and holding her sceptre in a manner and attitude which said, 'I have it, and none shall wrest it from me!' even Carlyle, who was standing near me, uttered with emotion, 'A blessing on her head.' "

It has been recorded that, after this tiring ceremony, the Queen gave a banquet at the Palace to a hundred guests; but this is hardly accurate, as no one was at dinner except those in the house, among whom were Her Majesty's half-brother and sister, and her future father-in-law, the Duke of Saxe-Coburg. The crowd was too great, indeed, for any one to have come, had they been invited. The Ministers gave official State dinners, and the Duke of Wellington a grand ball, to which 2,000 guests were invited; and a fair was held in Hyde Park, which lasted four days; the theatres were thrown open, and the whole of London was illuminated, the conduct of the crowds being excellent.

Of the routine of the Court after its return to Windsor in this year, Greville gives a full account: "The life which the Queen leads is this: She gets up soon after eight o'clock, breakfasts in her own room, and is employed the whole morning in transacting business; she reads all the dispatches, and has every matter of interest and importance in every department laid before her. At eleven or twelve Melbourne comes to her, and stays an hour, more or less, according to the business he may have to transact. At two she rides with a large suite (and she likes to have it numerous); Melbourne always rides on her left hand, and the enquerry-in-waiting generally on her right; after riding she amuses herself for the rest of the afternoon with music and singing, playing, romping with children, if there are any in the Castle (and she is so fond of them that she generally contrives to have some there), or in any other way she fancies. The hour for dinner is nominally half-past seven o'clock, soon after which time the guests assemble; but she seldom appears till near eight. When the guests are all assembled, the Queen comes in, preceded by the gentlemen of her household, and followed by the Duchess of Kent and all her ladies. She remains at table the usual time, but does not suffer the men to sit long after her, and we were summoned to coffee in less than a quarter of an hour. In the drawing-room she never sits down till the men make their appearance. Coffee is then served to them in the adjoining room, and then they go into the drawing-room, when she goes round and says a few words to each. When this little ceremony is over, the Duchess of Kent's whist table is arranged. At about half-past eleven Her Majesty goes to bed. This is the whole history of her day; she orders and regulates every detail herself; she knows where everybody is lodged in the Castle, settles about the riding or driving, and enters into every particular with minute attention." This regularity in allotment of time, and careful attention to every point of detail, both in her own household and the discharge of public duty, has been one of the marked characteristics of Her Majesty's life throughout the whole of her long reign. Even in its earliest days, she would refuse to sign a document declared to be of paramount importance without having mastered its contents; but the story, which has gained extensive currency, that once she replied to Lord Melbourne, who was urging the expediency of a measure, "I have been taught to judge between right and wrong, but expediency is a word I neither wish to hear nor to understand," is quite a myth. The last matter of importance before the great change in her life, to be told in the next chapter, was the fall and restoration of the Melbourne administration, when, on the question of the retirement with the Government of the Ladies of the Household, the firmness of the young Queen resulted in her retaining them in her service, and the Ministry remained practically unchanged.

CHAPTER FIVE.

On the 26th of August, 1819, almost exactly three months after the birth of the Princess Victoria of Kent, was born the second son of Ernest, Duke of Saxe-Coburg-Saalfeld, and of his wife, Louise, daughter of Augustus, Duke of Saxe-Gotha-Altenburg. He was born at Rosenau, a favorite Summer residence of his father, and received the names of Frances Albert Charles Augustus Emanuel. At his baptism an address was pronounced by the Superintendent Genzler, who had officiated the year before at the marriage of the Duke and Duchess of Kent at Coburg. In it occur two passages which are singularly prophetic of the after life of the infant Prince. "The good wishes," said the preacher, "with which we welcome this infant as a Christian, as one destined to be great on earth, and as a future heir to everlasting life, are the more earnest when we consider the high position in life in which he may one day be placed, and the sphere of action to which the will of God may call him, in order to contribute more or less to the promotion of truth and virtue, and to the extension of the Kingdom of God. * * * The thoughts and supplications of the loving mother are: that her beloved son may one day enter into the Kingdom of God, as pure and innocent after the trials of this life as he is at this moment (the joy and hope of his parents) received into the Communion of this Christian Church, whose vocation it is to bring up and form upon earth a God-fearing race." These words, spoken at his baptism, could not have been more descriptive of the Prince had they been used after his premature death.

The child received his first name of Francis from the Emperor of Austria. But he was always called by his second name, Albert, given him after a Duke of Saxe Teschen, an ancestor, whose branch of the family subsequently became extinct. Duke Ernest, the father of Prince Albert, succeeded his father, Francis Anthony, of Saxe-Coburg-Saalfeld, in 1806, and afterward, in 1826, by a redivision of the family titles and estates, became Duke of Saxe-Coburg and Gotha. The Duke's second brother, Ferdinand George, married the heiress of the Prince of Kohary, in Hungary, and their son became King Consort of Portugal by his marriage with Queen Donna Maria II. of that kingdom. The third brother was Leopold, King of the Belgians. Of the four daughters of Duke Francis, mention has been made in a preceding chapter.

As has been before stated, the union of the Prince with his cousin Victoria was the cherished hope of their common grandmother, who died when her grandchildren were only twelve years old; but their uncle, King Leopold, steadily pursued this plan, afterward crowned with such conspicuous success. The first meeting of the cousins has already been mentioned, and the strong affection entertained by the Queen for the Prince is shown by her letter to her uncle at the close of the visit to Kensington. The probability of the union was no secret at the time, though King William IV. preferred the idea of an alliance with Prince Albert of the Netherlands. But after the Queen's accession to the throne, rumors of her contemplated marriage with Prince Albert became general. It was in order to quiet these reports that, in the autumn of 1837, by the advice of the King of the Belgians, the Prince, with his brother Prince Ernest, went for a tour in Switzerland.

The Queen, alluding in 1864 to this tour, relates that that the Prince sent her a small book of sketches. "The whole of these were placed in a small album, with the dates at which each place was visited in the Prince's handwriting; and this album the Queen now considers one of her greatest treasures, and never goes anywhere without it. Nothing had at this time passed between the Queen and the Prince; but this gift shows that the latter, in the midst of his travels, often thought of his young cousin."

In the early part of the next year, the Prince paid a visit to his uncle Leopold at Brussels, when the King spoke to him fully about his future prospects. The King had already mentioned to the Queen the idea of the marriage, and the proposal must have been favorably entertained, for, in writing to Baron Stockmar, he alludes to the manner in which Prince Albert had received the communication which, of course with the Queen's consent, he had made to him. In his letters he expresses the very high opinion which he had formed of his nephew's character. "He looks at the question from its most elevated and honorable point of view; he considers that troubles are inseparable from all human positions, and that, therefore, if one must be subject to plagues and annoyances, it is better to be so for some great or worthy object, than for trifles and mis-

eries. I have told him that his great youth would make
it necessary to postpone the marriage for a few years."

The interval of postponement was not long. On the
8th of October, 1839, the Princes Ernest and Albert left
Brussels on the expedition which decided the fate of
the younger brother. At Windsor, two days later, they
were most cordially and affectionately received by the
Queen. Four days were spent in the usual manner, riding in the afternoon with dinner parties and sometimes
dances in the evening, and on the 14th the Queen, in
an interview with Lord Melbourne, told him that she
made up her mind to the marriage. He expressed great
satisfaction at the decision, and said to her, as Her
Majesty records in her journal, " 'I think it will be very
well received; for I hear that there is an anxiety now
that it should be, and I am very glad of it;' adding, in
quite a paternal tone, 'You will be much more comfortable; for a woman cannot stand alone for any time,
in whatever position she may be.' " Can we wonder
that the Queen, recalling these circumstances, should ex-
claim, "Alas alas! the poor Queen now stands in that
painful position!" An intimation was conveyed to the
Prince that the Queen wished to speak to him next
day, and, accordingly, soon after noon he obeyed the
summons to her room, where he found her alone.
After a few moments' conversation the Queen told him
why she had sent for him.

His old friend, Baron Stockmar, is thus informed by
by the Prince of his engagement, "I write to you on
one of the happiest days of my life to give you the most
welcome news possible." "Victoria is so good and kind
to me, that I am often puzzled to believe that I should
be the object of so much affection. I know the interest

you take in my happiness, and therefore pour out my heart to you. * * * More, or more seriously, I cannot write, I am at this moment too much bewildered to do so—

> " 'Heaven opens on the ravish'd eye,
> The heart is all entranced in bliss.' "

These lines are thus translated from Schiller's "Song of the Bell," by Sir Theodore Martin, in his Life of the Prince Consort, where more correspondence between the different members of the family, at this interesting time, is given at length.

It had been originally intended to communicate the approaching event to Parliament, when it assembled, in the ordinary course, at the beginning of the coming year. This intention was, however, subsequently abandoned. Writing to the King of the Belgians on the 29th of October, 1839, the Queen says: "Before I proceed further, I wish just to mention one or two alterations in the plan of announcing the event. As Parliament has nothing whatever to say respecting the marriage—can neither approve nor disapprove it (I mean in a manner which might affect it)—it is now proposed that, as soon as my cousins are gone (which they now intend to do on the 14th of November, as time presses), I should assemble all the Privy Council, and announce my intention to them."

Writing from Windsor at this time to Baron Stockmar, Prince Albert strikes, as it were, the keynote of his future career: "I have laid to heart your friendly and kind-hearted advice as to the true foundation on which my future happiness must rest, and it agrees entirely with the principles of action which I had already privately framed for myself. An individuality, a character, which shall win the respect, the love, and the confidence of the Queen and of the nation, must be the groundwork of my position. This individuality gives security for the disposition which prompts the actions; and even should mistakes occur, they will be more easily pardoned on account of that personal character; while even the most noble and beautiful undertakings fail in procuring support to a man who is not capable of inspiring that confidence. If therefore, I prove a 'noble' Prince, in the true sense of the word, as you call upon me to be, wise and prudent conduct will become easier to me, and its results more rich in blessings. I will not let my courage fail. With firm resolution and true zeal on my part, I cannot fail to continue 'noble, manly, and princely' in all things. In what I may do, good advice is the first thing necessary; and that you can give better than any one, if you can only make up your mind to sacrifice your time to me for the first year of my existence here."

In the same strain of thought, the devotion of all his own individual powers for the good and happiness of millions, he writes to his stepmother: "With the exception of my relations toward her (the Queen), my future position will have its dark sides, and the sky will not always be blue and unclouded. But life has its thorns in every position, and the consciousness of having used one's powers and endeavors for an object so great as that of promoting the good of so many, will surely be sufficient to support me."

Of the character of the Prince at this time, perhaps the best analysis is to be found in a letter addressed by Baron Stockmar to the Baroness Lehzen. It was important to give a proper estimate of him to the members of the Royal Household, and to show that, though so young, he was deserving of their admiration and respect. The letter is dated 15th of December, 1839. "With sincere pleasure I assure you the more I see of the Prince the better I esteem and love him. His intellect is so sound and clear, his nature so unspoiled, so childlike, so predisposed to goodness as well as truth, that only two external elements will be required to make of him a truly distinguished Prince. The first of these will be opportunity to acquire a proper knowledge of men and of the world; the second will be intercourse with Englishmen of experience, culture, and integrity, by whom he may be made thoroughly conversant with their Nation and Constitution. * * * As regards his future relation to the Queen, I have a confident hope that they will make each other happy by mutual love, confidence, and esteem. As I have known the Queen, she was always quick and acute in her perceptions, straightforward moreover, of singular purity of heart, without a trace of vanity or pretension. She will consequently do full justice to the Prince's hand and heart; and if this be so, and the Prince be really loved by the Queen, and recognized for what he is, then his position will be right in the main, especially if he manage at the same time to secure the good will of the Nation. Of course he will have storms to encounter, and disagreeables, like other people, especially those of exalted rank. But if he really possesses the love of the Queen and the respect of the Nation, I will answer for it that after every storm he will come safely into port. You will therfore have my entire approval, if you think the best course is to leave him to his clear head, his sound feeling and excellent disposition."

On the 20th of November, 1839, the Queen, who had already communicated to all the members of the Royal Family the news of her intended marriage, came up from Windsor to Buckingham Palace to confer with Lord Melbourne upon the form of the declaration to be made to the Privy Council at its meeting on the 23d. On that day the Council, upward of eighty in number, assembled in the bow-room at the Palace, where the Queen read the following declaration: "I have caused you to be summoned at the present time in order that I may acquaint you with my resolution in a matter which deeply concerns the welfare of my people, and the happiness of my future life. It is my intention to ally myself in marriage with the Prince Albert of Saxe-Coburg and Gotha. Deeply impressed with the solemnity of the engagement which I am about to contract, I have not come to this decision without mature consideration, nor without feeling a strong assurance that with the blessing of Almighty God it will at once secure my domestic felicity and serve the interests of my country.

"I have thought fit to make this resolution known to you at the earliest period, in order that you may be apprised of a matter so highly important to me and to my kingdom, and which, I persuade myself, will be most acceptable to all my loving subjects."

"Whereupon," it is stated in the Minutes of Council, "all the Privy Councillors present made it their humble request to Her Majesty that Her Majesty's most gracious declaration to them might be made public; which Her Majesty was pleased to order accordingly."

The announcement of the forthcoming marriage was hailed with great rejoicing through the country. Mixed with the cordial sympathy felt by the people with the prospect of the happiness of their beloved sovereign, was a feeling of profound satisfaction at the removal of all uncertainty as to the object of the Queen's choice.

During the period immediately following the declaration, precedents were searched for bearing on the Prince's position and the composition of his household. Unfortunately the precedent commonly referred to was that of Prince George of Denmark, the husband of Queen Anne, who was a Peer, and also for some time Lord High Admiral of England. Prince Albert, however, as had been previously decided between the Queen and himself, refused every title. Other matters, too, had to be discussed, such as the naturalization of the Prince, the formation of his household, and the income which was to be settled upon him. This last matter and the question of his precedence were not arranged without some difficulty and annoyance. On the 16th of January, 1840, the Queen opened Parliament in person, meeting a most enthusiastic reception from the crowds which had assembled along the route from the Palace to the Houses of Parliament, the Queen herself recording in her journal that she "was more loudly cheered than she had been for some time." The House itself was densely thronged, and the whole assemblage was deeply touched at hearing the youthful sovereign, with her clear voice and distinct articulation, announcing to the assembled Parliament her own approaching marriage.

"Since you were last assembled, I have declared my intention of allying myself in marriage with the Prince Albert of Saxe-Coburg and Gotha. I humbly implore that the Divine blessing may prosper this union, and render it conducive to the interests of my people, as well as to my own domestic happiness; and it will be to me a source of the most lively satisfaction to find the resolution I have taken approved by my Parliament.

"The constant proofs which I have received of your attachment to my person and family, persuade me that you will enable me to provide for such an establishment as may appear suitable to the rank of the Prince, and the dignity of the Crown."

In answer to the Queen's speech, loyal addresses were moved in both Houses. Sir Robert Peel, as leader of the Opposition, joined heartily in the congratulations offered by the address, saying: "I do entirely enter into the aspirations for the happiness of Her Majesty in her approaching nuptials. * * * Her Majesty has the singular good fortune to be able to gratify her private feelings while she performs her public duty, and to obtain the best guarantee for happiness by contracting an alliance founded on affection. I cordially hope that the union now contemplated will contribute to Her Majesty's happiness, and enable her to furnish to her people an exalted example of connubial felicity."

Cordial, however, though the general feeling of both Houses was as to the intended marriage, the omission of any mention of the Prince's religion from the Queen's speech was the subject of debate in the Upper House; and in the House of Commons a long and heated discussion arose on the proposal to grant an annual sum of £50,000 to Prince Albert on his marriage. The amount of the grant was finally fixed at £30,000, much to the annoyance of the Queen, and to the disappointment of the Prince, who had looked forward to the prospect of being able to promote the interests of literature, science, and art in a more generous manner than his reduced income permitted. From the first he rose superior to anything like personal considerations, and his future relations with the leaders of the party by whose means the vote was reduced, showed how little his conduct was influenced by these political quarrels.

A more mortifying event, occurring on the same day in the House of Lords, was the defeat of the Government on the question of the precedence to be granted in this country to the Prince. The Queen, in her journal, says that she was most indignant at what had occurred, and that it cannot be wondered at that the first impression made on the Prince's mind should have been a most painful one. But, as has already been said, he soon understood the nature of our political parties, and recognized that the proceedings in Parliament were only the result of high party feeling, and were by no means to be taken as marks of personal disrespect or of want of kind feeling to himself. For details of these controversies and the feeling they produced, the reader is referred to Sir Theodore Martin's Life of the Prince Consort. The immediate result was an order in Council which settled the Prince's position as following next after that of the Queen.

The news of these debates in the Houses of Parliament met the Prince on his way to England at Aix. He was naturally somewhat disturbed, but remarks in his letter to the Queen, "All I have to say is, that, while I possess your love, they cannot make me unhappy." Any misgiving as to his popularity must, however, have been dispelled by the warmth of his reception at Dover, where he landed on the 6th of February, 1840, and by the enthusiastic greeting which welcomed him along his journey through Kent till he reached Buckingham Palace on the 8th.

The marriage was fixed for one o'clock on the 10th at the Chapel Royal, St. James's, and at half-past twelve the Queen left Buckingham Palace with the Duchess of Kent and the Mistress of the Robes, the Duchess of Sutherland. The morning had been dark and dismal, with rain and fog. The Prince, who was supported by his father, the Duke of Saxe-Coburg and Gotha, and by his brother Ernest, had preceded the Queen to the chapel. He wore the Garter, and the Star of the Order in brilliants which had been presented to him the day before by the Queen. After a short interval, to the strains of the National Anthem, the procession of the bride entered. The Queen was preceded by the members of the Royal Family and the officers of State, the sword of State being carried before Her Majesty by Lord Melbourne. She wore a wreath of orange blossoms, and round her shoulders the collar of the Garter. Her train was borne by twelve bridesmaids, daughters of peers. They were the Lady Adelaide Paget, Lady Caroline Gordon Lennox, Lady Sarah Villiers, Lady Elizabeth Howard, Lady Frances Cowper, Lady Ida Hay, Lady Elizabeth West, Lady Catherine Stanhope, Lady Mary Grimston, Lady Jane Bouverie, Lady Eleanora Paget, and Lady Mary Howard. The ceremony was performed by the Archbishop of Canterbury, and the royal bride was given away by the Duke of Sussex. A large picture of the ceremony was painted by Sir George Hayter, the principal group from which has been reproduced in the plate opposite page 68. It is taken at the moment when the Queen accompanied her promise to "love, honor and obey," with the look of love and trust which assured the spectators that her heart was in her words. At the instant when the ring was placed on her finger, the signal was given for firing the guns which communicated to the whole city the glad news of the union of the sovereign with the husband of her choice. The scene, as the newly married pair left the chapel, has been described by the Dowager Lady Lyttelton, one of the ladies-in-waiting, who, writing a few days afterward, says: "The Queen's look and manner were very pleasing; great happiness in her countenance; and her look of confidence and comfort at the Prince, when they walked away as man and wife, was very pleasing to see. I understand she is in extremely high spirits since. Such a new thing for her to dare to be unguarded in conversing with anybody; and with her frank and fearless nature, the restraints she has hitherto been under from one reason or another must have been most painful."

After the conclusion of the ceremony the Queen and Prince Albert, with the members of the Royal Family and the principal Ministers of State, passed into the throne-room. Here the marriage register was signed. By special permission a fac-simile of the document is given on the opposite page. These signatures were attested by the Queen Adelaide and others present to the number of twenty-one; the Duke of Wellington's name does not appear, though it has often been said that he was one of the signatories. The united procession then returned to Buckingham Palace, the Queen being accompanied in her carriage by her husband alone. After the wedding breakfast the newly married pair started for Windsor; the sun, as they left the Palace, bursting through the clouds—an omen of brightness and happiness for the future. Windsor was reached in the evening, where the reception was no less loyal and enthusiastic than had been the greetings of the populace in London.

On the 28th of February the Duke of Coburg left England. The separation was keenly felt by the Prince. "He said to me," the Queen records in her Journal, "that I had never known a father, and could not therefore feel what he did. His childhood had been very happy. Ernest, he said, was now the only one remaining here of all his earliest ties and recollections; but that if I continued to love him as I did now, I could make up for all. * * * Oh, how I did feel for my dearest, precious husband at this moment. Father, brother, friends, country—all has he left, and all for me. God grant that I may be the happy person, the most happy person,. to make this dearest, blessed being happy and contented! What is in my power to make him happy I will do."

CHAPTER SIX.

MARRIED LIFE; 1840-52.

Loyalty claims much from, and lays heavy burdens on, those who have to sustain its duties and responsibilities. Little time can be given to rest and repose, and in the case of the Queen and Prince Albert the privacy, which newly married subjects are privileged to enjoy for weeks, was, after four short days, exchanged for the routine of State ceremonial and public business. The Court returned to London on the 14th of February, and addresses were received both by the Queen and the Prince from the two Houses of Parliament, and other bodies. In the evenings State dinners were given, and visits paid to the theatres. On the 19th the first levee was held, at which the Prince, as on all subsequent occasions, led the Queen in, and stood on her left hand. On the 17th of March the Prince received and personally answered no less than twenty-seven addresses. In writing to his grandmother, he remarks: "It is not to be told what a quantity of presentations I have, and how many people I must become acquainted with. I cannot yet quite remember their faces, but this will come right. After the last levee, Victoria gave me the Order of the Bath." The Prince had already received the Garter, and had been made a Field-Marshal in the British Army. He was, in addition, appointed Colonel of the Eleventh Regiment of Light Dragoons, which regiment then received and still bears the title of Prince Albert's Own Hussars.

His Royal Highness' Household had also by this time been appointed. On this subject he had expressed a very earnest wish in a letter to the Queen on the 10th of December, 1839: "Now I come to a second point which you touch upon in your letter, and which I have also much at heart; I mean the choice of the persons who are to belong to my household. The maxim, 'Tell me whom he associates with, and I will tell you who he is,' must here especially not be lost sight of. I should wish particularly that the selection should be made without regard to politics; for if I am really to keep myself free from all parties, my people must not belong exclusively to one side. Above all, these appointments should not be mere 'party rewards,' but they should possess other recommendations besides those of party. Let them be either of any high rank, or very rich, or very clever, or persons who have performed important services for England. It is very necessary that they should be chosen from both sides—the same number of Whigs as of Tories; and above all do I wish that they should be well-educated men, and of high character, who, as I have already said, shall have already distinguished themselves in their several positions, whether it be in the Army, or Navy, or in the scientific world. I know you will agree with my views."

The Prince's household consisted of a Groom of the Stole, of two Lords-in-Waiting, two Equerries, afterward increased to four, two Grooms-in-Waiting, and a Private Secretary. These officers were appointed on the principle which was observed in the Queen's household, namely, that those appointments only should be permanent which were held by men entirely unconnected with politics. This regulation, however, only affected the Groom of the Stole, Lord Robert Grosvenor (afterward Lord Ebury), and one of the Lords-in-Waiting. The nomination of Mr. Anson as Private Secretary was not made without considerable hesitation, and was consented to by the Prince with reluctance, on the ground that, as Mr. Anson had been for some time Private Secretary to Lord Melbourne, his appointment to so confidential a post might seem inconsistent with the entire freedom from partisanship which the Prince had desired should be observed in the formation of his household. The appointment, however, proved singularly satisfactory. Mr. Anson's straightforward conduct and absolute devotion to the service and interests of his master soon won the entire confidence and friendship of Prince Albert. His sudden death at a later date deeply affected the Prince, who said to the Queen, "He was my only intimate friend in this country. We went through everything together since I came here. He was almost like a brother to me."

Up to this time her mother had been the Queen's constant companion. But on the 13th of April Her Royal Highness removed to Ingestre House, Belgrave Square. Here the Duchess lived till after the death of the Princess Augusta, when she moved to Clarence House, St. James', which for the rest of her life was her London home. At the same time Frogmore House, which became vacant from the same cause, was also assigned to the Duchess, who, when the Court was at Windsor, came over almost daily to lunch or dine with the Queen.

Easter, 1840, was spent at Windsor, and for the first time the Queen and Prince received the Sacrament together in St. George's Chapel. "The Prince," the Queen says, "had a very strong feeling about the solemnity of this act, and did not like to appear in company either the evening before or on the day on which he took it, and he and the Queen almost always dined alone on these occasions." The Queen notes this strong feeling on the part of the Prince more than once in her Journal for 1840 and 1841. On another occasion, a few months later, about Christmas time, when they again took the Sacrament in the private chapel at Windsor, she says: "We two dined together, as Albert likes being quite alone before he takes the Sacrament; we played part of Mozart's Requiem, and then he read to me out of the Stunden der Andacht (Hours of Devotion) the article on Selbsterkenntniss (Self-knowledge)."

On the 23d of May, the Queen and Prince went to Claremont to keep Her Majesty's birthday in private. This continued to be the Queen's custom till 1848, when Claremont was given up to the exiled royal family of France. In later years the birthday was passed at Osborne, but since 1861 the Queen has usually spent the day at Balmoral.

On the 10th of June, 1840, an event occurred which created intense excitement throughout the country. While the Queen and Prince were driving in the afternoon along Constitution Hill on their way to Hyde Park, a young man named Edward Oxford advanced within a few yards of the carriage, and fired a pistol at the Queen. He missed his aim, but, as the carriage proceeded on its way, the would-be assassin called out, "I have another," and discharged a second pistol, again without effect. The Queen's first thought was for her mother, and, changing her route to Belgrave Square, the Duchess of Kent heard of the attempt and of her daughter's safety at the same moment.

On leaving Ingestre House and driving through the Park on their return to the Palace, the Queen and the Prince were received by an immense crowd, which had collected on hearing the news, with enthusiastic demonstration of loyalty and rejoicing at the escape of their sovereign. The trial of Oxford for high treason was held in the Central Criminal Court on the 8th of July. The jury returned the verdict of "Not guilty on the ground of insanity," and the prisoner was therefore ordered to be detained during Her Majesty's pleasure. After thirty-five years' imprisonment at Bedlam and Dartmoor, he was released on condition that he would emigrate to Australia.

About the same time, the prospect of an heir to the throne rendered it expedient to provide for the possibilities of the death of the Queen, and of a prolonged minority. The question of a Regency had therefore to be considered. The Queen, in her Journal, says: "A Council of Regency was first suggested; but when Lord Melbourne spoke to the Duke of Wellington, he immediately answered for himself, 'that it could and ought to be nobody but the Prince.'" A bill for the purpose was brought in and passed with only one dissentient voice, that of the Duke of Sussex. On the 2d of August the Prince writes: "The Regency Bill has passed safely through all its stages, and is now conclusively settled. * * * It is very gratifying that not a single voice was raised in opposition in either House, or in any one of the newspapers." And this was more gratifying, as Lord Melbourne told the Queen it was entirely owing to the golden opinions the Prince had won everywhere since his arrival. "Three months ago," Lord Melbourne said to the Queen, "they would not have done it for him;" adding, the Queen writes in her Journal, "with tears in his eyes, 'it is entirely his own character.' "

On the 11th of August the Queen porogued Parliament in person, and next day the Court left London for Windsor, where the Queen and Prince received the King and Queen of the Belgians, the Princess Hohenlohe and her children, and Queen Adelaide. A short visit was paid in September to Claremont, at the time of the death of Princess Augusta, in order to be away at the time of Her Royal Highness' funeral, which, on account of the Queen's health, the Prince could not attend.

On the 13th of November 1840, the Court returned to Buckingham Palace, and there, on the 21st, the Queen's first-born saw the light. In a letter to his father, on the 23d, the Prince writes: "The little one is very well and very merry. * * * I should certainly have liked it better if she had had a son, as would Victoria also; but, at the same time, we must be equally satisfied and thankful as it is. * * * The rejoicing in the public is universal."

"For a moment only," the Queen says, "was he disappointed at its being a daughter, and not a son. His first thought was for the safety of the Queen, and during the time she was laid up, his care and devotion were quite beyond expression."

During the Queen's illness the Prince, who, in the previous September, had been introduced into the Privy Council, saw the ministers, and transacted all necessary business for her. From the very first, the Queen, on the advice of Lord Melbourne, had communicated all dispatches on foreign affairs to the Prince, who, writing to his father, says: "I think I have already done some good. I always commit my views to paper, and then communicate them to Lord Melbourne. He seldom answers me, but I have often had the satisfaction of seeing him act entirely in accordance with what I have said." Again, in 1841, when the Eastern Question was approaching a crisis, the Prince writes: "I study the politics of the day with great industry. I speak quite openly with the Ministers on all subjects, so as to gain information. * * * And I endeavor quietly to be of as much use to Victoria in her position as I can."

The Prince had, in fact, already qualified himself to render the Queen invaluable service in the political crisis that was now rapidly approaching. On the 23d of June, 1841, Parliament had been dissolved. But the elections went against the Government, who, on August the 28th, were defeated in the new Parliament by a majority of 91, in the debate on the address. Two days later the Ministry resigned. In thus resigning, Lord Melbourne had the consolation of feeling that he left a devoted, sagacious, and permanent counsellor at the Queen's side. "For four years," he said, "I have seen you every day; but it is so different now to what it would have been in 1839. The Prince understands everything so well, and has a clever, able head." The Queen, as she records in her Journal, saw Lord Melbourne before he left the Castle, and was much affected in taking leave of him. "You will find," he said, "a great support in the Prince; he is so able. You said when you were going to be married that he was perfection, which I thought a little exaggerated then, but really I think now that it is in some degree realized." And a few days afterwards, writing to King Leopold, Her Majesty says: "I cannot say what a comfort and support my beloved Albert is to me—how well and how kindly and properly he behaves. I cannot resist copying for you what Lord Melbourne wrote to me about him, the evening after we parted. He had already praised him greatly to me before he took leave of me. It is as follows: 'Lord Melbourne cannot satisfy himself without again stating to Your Majesty in writing what he had the honor of saying to Your Majesty respecting His Royal Highness, the Prince. Lord Melbourne has formed the highest opinion of His Royal Highness' judgment, temper, and discretion, and he cannot but feel a great consideration and security in the reflection that he leaves Your Majesty in a situation in which Your Majesty has the inestimable advantage of such advice and assistance. Lord Melbourne feels certain that Your Majesty cannot do better than have recourse to it whenever it is needed, and rely upon it with confidence.' This naturally gave me great pleasure, and made me very proud, as it comes from a person who is no flatterer, and would not have said it if he did not think so or feel so."

The same impression of ability was made by the Prince, in the early years of his married life, on the succeeding Minister. Sir Robert Peel, writes Lord Kingsdown in his Recollections (quoted by Sir Theodore Martin), "when he introduced me to him in 1841, said that I should find him one of the most extraordinary young men I had ever met with. So," adds Lord Kingsdown, "it proved. His aptitude for business was wonderful; the dullest and most intricate matters did not escape or weary his attention; his judgment was very good; his readiness to listen to any suggestions, though against his own opinions, was constant; and though I saw his temper very often tried, yet in the course of twenty years, I never once saw it disturbed, nor witnessed any signs of impatience."

On the 10th of February, 1841, the first anniversary of the marriage of her parents, the infant Princess Royal was christened at Buckingham Palace. A new silver-gilt font had been provided for the occasion, richly ornamented with the arms of the Princess and her father and mother—a font which has always since been used for royal baptisms to the present day. The water used on the occasion was brought from the river Jordan. The ceremony was performed by the Archbishop of Canterbury, who was assisted by the Archbishop of York, the Bishops of London and Norwich, and the Dean of Carlisle. The sponsors were Queen Adelaide, the Duchess of Gloucester, the Duchess of Kent, the King of the Belgians, the Duke of Sussex, and the Duke of Saxe-Coburg and Gotha, who was represented by the Duke of Wellington. The names, "Victoria Adelaide Mary Louisa," were given to the infant by Queen Adelaide. Prince Albert wrote to the Dowager-Duchess of Gotha, "The christening went off very well; your little great-granddaughter behaved with great propriety and like a Christian. She was awake but did not cry at all, and seemed to crow with immense satisfaction at the lights and brilliant uniforms, for she is very intelligent and observing. The ceremony took place at half-past six p. m. After it there was a dinner, and then we had some instrumental music. The health of the little one was drunk with great enthusiasm."

It was in this year that the Queen had the great satisfaction of seeing Prince Albert placed at the head of the Royal Commission, appointed to promote and encourage in the United Kingdom that study of the fine arts for which a unique opportunity was afforded by the building of the new Houses of Parliament. To fill such a post the Prince was exceptionally fitted. King Leopold in his "Reminiscences," in writing of his own father, says: "His great love and knowledge of everything connected with the fine arts was inherited by Albert. No one else in the family possessed it to the same degree." The chairmanship of this Commission brought the Prince into connection with the leading public and literary men of the country, and he followed up the connection with characteristic energy and ability. By constant and unremitting labor he was able to influence, more than any single man, the movement which, from this date and through the Great Exhibition of 1851, raised the artistic level of the country from the depths in which it had previously stagnated.

At this time the Queen and the Prince were both practising the art of etching, under the able tuition of Mr., afterward Sir Edwin, Landseer, one of the few English artists of the day of brilliant and original genius. In quantity their work was necessarily limited by the pressure of important business; but in quality it was excellent, and the precision of drawing and neatness of execution in the plates, which were all bitten in under their own supervision, have always excited the admiration of those who possess, or have seen, these interesting productions.

On the 9th of November, 1841, a male heir was born to the throne. The event was announced by a Gazette Extraordinary, dated "Buckingham Palace, November 9th. This morning, at twelve minutes before eleven o'clock, the Queen was happily delivered of a Prince, His Royal Highness, Prince Albert, Her Royal Highness the Duchess of Kent, several Lords of Her Majesty's most honorable Privy Council, and the Ladies of Her Majesty's Bedchamber being present. This great and important news was immediately made known to the town by the firing of the Park and Tower guns; and the Privy Council being assembled as soon as possible thereupon, at he Council Chamber, Whitehall, it was ordered that a Form of Thanksgiving for the Queen's safe delivery of a Prince be prepared by His Grace the Archbishop of Canterbury, to be used in all churches and chapels throughout England and Wales, and the town of Berwick-upon-Tweed, on Sunday the 14th of November, or the Sunday after the respective ministers shall receive the same. Her Majesty and the infant Prince are, God be praised, both doing well." Successive bulletins confirmed the glad news of the convalescence of Her Majesty and of the health of the Prince. The only drawback to the national rejoicing was the serious illness of the Queen Adelaide, who lay in a very critical state, from which, in the course of a short time, she happily recovered.

The news of the birth of the Prince nowhere created more excitement and satisfaction than in the city of London, where the citizens were engaged in celebrating the inauguration of their chief magistrate, and the Lord Mayor and the authorities immediately proceeded in great state to the Palace to tender their loyal congratulations to their sovereign. The Prince, who was born Duke of Cornwall and Duke of Rothesay, was shortly afterward created, by letters patent, Prince of Wales and Earl of Chester.

The Queen's recovery was so rapid that, on the 6th of December, the Court removed to Windsor. "We arrived here sains et saufs," writes the Queen to King Leopold, "with our awfully large nursery establishment yesterday morning. I wonder very much whom our little boy will be like. You will understand how fervent are my prayers, and I am sure everybody's must be, to see him resemble his father in every, every respect, both in body and mind! Oh, my dearest uncle, I am sure if you knew how happy, how blessed I feel, and how proud in possessing such a perfect being as my husband, and if you think that you have been instrumental in bringing about this union, it must gladden your heart!" Again, on the 14th of December, the Queen continues, "We must all have trials and vexations, but if one's home is happy then the rest is comparatively nothing. I assure you, dear uncle, that no one feels this more than I do. I had this autumn one of the severest trials I could have, in parting with my government, and particularly from one kind and valued friend, and I feel even now this last very much: but my happiness at home, the love of my husband, his kindness, his advice, his support and his company make up for all, and make me forget it."

On the 25th of January, 1842, the Prince of Wales was christened in St. George's Chapel at Windsor. The choice of sponsors was not easy. The difficulty was met by inviting the King of Prussia to undertake the office. Though not connected with the parents by the tie of blood, his position as sovereign of the most important Protestant kingdom on the Continent justified the selection. King Frederic William, who had long been anxious to visit England, accepted the invitation. Arriving at Greenwich on the 22d, he proceeded at once to Windsor. Royal baptisms had been hitherto, as a rule, celebrated within the Palace; but in the special circumstances, it was considered expedient that the heir to the throne should be christened in a consecrated and historical building. No fitter shrine for the purpose could have been chosen than the regal chapel which was raised in honor of, and dedicated to, the Patron Saint of the land. The rite was performed at ten a. m., with great state and splendor. Besides the King of Prussia, the other sponsors were the Duchess of Saxe-Coburg, represented by the Duchess of Kent, the Duke of Cambridge, the Duchess of Saxe-Gotha, represented by the Duchess of Cambridge, the Princess Sophia, represented by the Princess Augusta of Cambridge, and Prince Ferdinand of Saxe-Coburg. The principal group around the font, which is that mentioned previously as made for the christening of the Princess Royal, is represented on the opposite page, in the reproduction taken from the large picture painted in commemoration of the event by Sir George Hayter. The Queen, in her Journal, says: "It is impossible to describe how beautiful and imposing the effect of the whole scene was in the fine old chapel, with the banners, the music, and the light shining on the altar."

The King of Prussia remained in this country for a fortnight, and on the 3d of February, the day before his departure, he was present at the opening of Parliament by the Queen in person. Of this brilliant scene the Baroness Bunsen gives a graphic account in a letter quoted in her husband's Memoirs: "On Thursday was the opening of Parliament—the great scene from which I had expected most, and was not disappointed. The throngs in the streets, in the windows, on every spot where foot could stand—all looking so pleased—the splendid Horse Guards, the Grenadier Guards—of whom it might be said, as the King did on another occasion, 'an appearance so fine you know not how to believe it true'—the Yeoman of the Body Guard; then in the House of Lords, the Peers in their robes, the beautifully dressed ladies, with many, many beautiful faces; last the procession of the Queen's entry, and herself, looking worthy and fit to be the converging point of so many rays of grandeur. * * * The composure with which she filled the throne, while awaiting the Commons, was a test of character—no fidget and no apathy. Then her voice and her enunciation could not be more perfect. In short, it could be said that she did well, but she was the Queen; she was, and felt herself to be, the acknowledged chief among grand national realities. Placed in a narrow space behind Her Majesty's mace-bearers, and peeping over their shoulders, I was enabled to hide and subdue the emotion I felt, in consciousness of the mighty pages of the world's history condensed in the words, so impressively uttered in the silver tones of that feminine voice—Peace and War, the fate of millions, relations of countries, exertions of power felt to the extremities of the globe, alterations of corn laws, the birth of a future sovereign—mentioned in solemn thankfulness to Him in whose hands are nations and rulers! With what should one respond, but with the heartfelt aspiration, 'God bless and guide her! for her sake, and the sake of all!'"

At the time of this opening of Parliament, the condition of home and foreign affairs was very serious. Scarcity of work inflicted widespread suffering on the manufacturing districts; riots among the workers in the iron and coal industries, and the risings threatened by Chartist agitators, caused deep anxiety to the ministry, whose powers of dealing with disturbances at home were enfeebled by the drain of troops required for operations abroad. The country was at war with China; in the West Indies and at the Cape the authorities needed all the help that could be spared; in Afghanistan a life and death struggle was raging, in which the British army had already met with the terrible disaster of the Cabul Pass; and in every quarter the outlook was full of menace and danger. A falling revenue demanded bold measures of finance, and the Queen cordially concurred in the proposal of Sir Robert Peel to impose an income tax, a step never before taken except under the pressure of a war expenditure, and always to the last degree unpopular. The Queen authorized her Ministers to announce that it was her wish not to be exempt from the operation of the tax, and this announcement was not without effect in reconciling her subjects to an impost previously unknown to that generation.

In order to revive the trade in London, every effort was made by the Court to stimulate its depressed condition. Dinners, concerts, and balls were frequently given, and on the 7th of May, with the same object, a grand costume ball was held in Buckingham Palace. At this the Queen appeared as Queen Philippa and the Prince as Edward III. Most of the guests wore costumes of the same date. The dress of the Queen was of Spitafields manufacture. On the 26th, the Queen and Prince went in state to a ball given at Covent Garden Theatre on behalf of the distressed Spitafields weavers. Fancy balls were also held at Apsley House and at

Stafford House with the same charitable object.

On the 29th of May, 1842, an attempt on the Queen's life, repeated by him next day, was made by a man named John Francis. An account of this outrage, confirmed by the Prince as authentic, has been given by Col. Arbuthnot, one of the equerries. "On Sunday, the 29th of May, at about two p. m., as Her Majesty alighted from her carriage at Buckingham Palace on her return from church, she spoke to Prince Albert, and on His Royal Highness entering the Palace he called me aside, and stated to me that a man in the crowd had presented a pistol toward the carriage, and he distinctly heard the noise, the same as the shutting of a pocketknife. His Royal Highness suggested to me the importance of keeping this a profound secret, but at once to consult the Inspector of Police. * * * In the evening Sir James Graham arrived, and he, Sir R. Peel, Col. Rowan and I went into a lower drawing room, where Sir Robert wrote down His Royal Highness' deposition to him. It was then fully agreed on the vital importance of our keping the matter a profound secret. * * * Her Majesty determined on the afternoon of Monday to drive out. I took every possible precaution, and His Royal Highness directed me to ride close to Her Majesty, and to request Col. Wylde to do the same, but His Royal Highness was so alive to the importance that the attempt on Sunday afternoon should be perfectly secret that he desired me not to mention it even to him. Her Majesty appeared to be as fully alive as I was to the danger she was incurring, but was, nothwithstanding, most calm, cheerful and composed, at the same time, I am sure, fully alive to the probability that from behind every tree she might be shot at. His Royal

Highness, I know, was fully conscious this might be the case.

"I had a strong feeling that, as the man had failed, and could not be aware that he was seen, he would take the earliest opportunity of renewing the attempt; so strong was my feeling, that I went myself to the stables to desire that on no account might Kangaroo be sent for me to ride, as he was a sluggish horse, and difficult to keep near the carriage, but notwithstanding, to my horror, Kangaroo was sent for me to ride and too late for me to change. The Queen drove through Hyde Park, the Regent's Park, and to Hampstead. I got, as soon as we were out of observation, on my groom's horse, and then I experienced a relief I cannot express, as I was able then to keep close to Her Majesty. We went fast home, but on passing through the gate at Constitution Hill, I desired the wheel postillion to drive even faster, which he did. Before arriving at the pump, I observed a man seemingly eager to see the Queen; on approaching him he snatched a pistol out of his breast and leveling quickly, aimed at the Queen, but owing to the rapid pace at which we were going, my horse being very near him, he was disconcerted, and by the mercy of Providence, aimed too low. Her Majesty heard the report, and her extraordinary calmness was wonderful. She was naturally affected, but did not betray the slightest appearance of alarm, but was as calm and as collected as when looking at the view at Hampstead. * * * His Royal Majesty struck me as being very much affected at Her Majesty's providential escape. On seeing the man after he had fired, His Royal Highness exclaimed: 'It is the same man.' "

Prince Albert, in his letter to his father, describing the

occurrence, says: "The shot must have passed under the carriage, for he lowered his hand. We felt as if a load had been taken off our hearts, and we thanked the Almighty for having preserved us a second time from so great a danger. John Francis (that is the man's name) was standing near a policeman, who immediately seized him, but could not prevent the shot. It was at the same spot where Oxford had fired at us, two years ago, with this difference only, that Oxford was standing on our left, with his back to the garden wall."

Mr. Anson, the Prince's Secretary, in his memoranda of the same day, says: "Her Majesty seemed none the worse. She told me she had fully expected it, and it was a relief to her to have it over. She had for some time been under the impression that one of these mad attempts would be made. * * * Her Majesty said she never could have existed under the uncertainty of a concealed attack. She would rather run the immediate risk at any time than have the presentiment of danger constantly hovering over her. She had been much gratified by the kind feeling people had shown." Contrary to her usual custom, she had on this day dispensed with the attendance of her ladies. To Miss Liddell, afterward Lady Bloomfield, the Queen said on her return to the Palace: "I daresay, Georgy, you were surprised at not driving with me this afternoon, but the fact was that as we returned from church yesterday, a man presented a pistol at the carriage window, which flashed in the pan; we were so taken by surprise that he had time to escape; so I knew what was hanging over me, and I was determined to expose no life but my own."

Francis was examined before the Privy Council and committed to Newgate for trial at the next session of the

Central Criminal Court. On the day following the attempt, an immense concourse of people assembled at the Palace in expectation that the Queen would take her accustomed drive. Nor were they disappointed. The royal carriage contained the Queen and Prince with the Duke of Saxe-Meiningen. Following on horseback were the Count Mensdorff with his four sons, and the two equerries. The royal party was loudly cheered, and the drive was quite a triumphal progress; Her Majesty's subjects appreciating with delight not only the presence of mind displayed by their youthful sovereign at the moment of danger, but the nerve with which she could go to meet it. The Queen, writing to King Leopold, says: "I was not really at all frightened, and feel very proud at dear Uncle Mensdorff calling me 'very courageous,' which I shall ever remember with delight, coming from so distinguished an officer as he is." In the evening the Queen, with Prince Albert, went to the Italian opera, where the audience, with tumultuous gratulations, called for the National Anthem, bursting into cheers at almost every line. On the day following address of congratulations were voted by both Houses of Parliament, followed by others from all parts of the kingdom.

Francis was tried for high treason on the 17th of June, found guilty, and sentenced to death. The Queen was most anxious that the sentence should not be carried out, and the Government, after consultation with the judges, commuted the sentence to transportation for life. The very next day after this exercise of clemency, another outrage was attempted, as the Queen, with the King of the Belgians, was driving to the Chapel Royal, St. James'. A deformed youth, named Bean, pointed a pistol at the Queen, but it fortunately missed fire, nor did the Queen know anything of the matter till her return to Buckingham Palace. On being told of it, she merely said that, so long as the law remained that these attempts could only be dealt with as acts of high treason, a recurrence of them must be expected. The Ministry, therefore, with as much haste as possible, brought in a bill making these attempts high misdemeanors, to be punished by transportation for seven years, or imprisonment, with, or without, hard labor, for a term not exceeding three years, the culprit "to be publicly, or privately, whipped, as often, and in such manner and form, as the Court shall direct, not exceeding thrice." The bill became law on the 16th of July, and under it Bean was, on August 25th, sentenced to eighteen months' imprisonment.

At Buckingham Palace, in the Summer of 1842, the Queen and Prince Albert had received Mendelssohn. The celebrated musician has given graphic details of his visit. He says in his letter to his mother: "I must tell you all the details of my last visit to Buckingham Palace. It is, as G. says, the one really pleasant and comfortable English house where one feels a son aise. Of course, I do know a few others, but yet, on the whole, I agreed with him. Prince Albert had asked me to go to him on Saturday at two o'clock, so that I might try his organ before I left England. I found him alone, and, as we were walking away, the Queen came in, also alone, in a simple morning dress. * * * I begged that the Prince would first play me something, so that, as I said, I might boast about it in Germany; and he played a chorale, by heart, with the pedals, so charmingly and clearly, and correctly, that it would have done credit to any professional. * * * Then it was my turn, and I began my Chorus from St. Paul, 'How Lovely Are the Messengers.' Before I got to the end of the first verse they both joined in the chorus; and all the time Prince Albert managed the stops for me so cleverly—first a flute, at the forte the great organ, at the D major part of the whole; then he made a lovely diminuendo with the stops, and so on to the end of the piece, and all by heart, that I was really quite enchanted. * * * The Queen asked if I had written any new songs, and said she was very fond of singing my published ones. 'You should sing one to him,' said Prince Albert; and, after a little begging, she said she would try the "Fruhlingslied" in B flat, 'if it is still here,' she added, 'for all my music is packed up for Claremont.' Prince Albert went to look for it, but came back saying it was already packed. * * * The servants were sent after it, without success; at last the Queen went herself, and, while she was gone, Prince Albert said to me: 'She begs you will accept this present as a remembrance,' and gave me a little case with a beautiful ring, on which is engraved—'V. R., 1842.'

"Then the Queen came back, and said: 'Lady —— is gone, and has taken all my things with her. It really is most annoying.' I then begged that I might not be made to suffer for the accident, and hoped she would sing another song. After some consultation with her husband, he said: 'She will sing you something of Gluck's. * * * We proceeded to the Queen's sitting-room, where there was a piano. The Duchess of Kent came in, and, while they were all talking, I rum-

maged about amongst the music, and soon discovered
my first set of songs. So, of course, I begged her rather
to sing one of those than the Gluck, to which she kindly
consented; and which did she choose?—'Schoner und
Schoner Schmuckt Sich!'—sang it quite charmingly in
strict time and tune, and with very good execution
* * * the last G I have never heard better or purer,
or more natural, from any amateur. Then, I was obliged
to confess that Fanny had written the song (which I
found very hard, but pride must have a fall), and begged
her to sing one of my own also. If I would give her
plenty of help, she would gladly try, she said; and then
she sang the Pilgerspruch, 'Las Dich Nur,' really quite
faultlessly, and with charming feeling and expression. I
thought to myself, one must not pay too many compli-
ments on such an occasion, so I merely thanked her a
great many times, upon which she said: 'Oh, if I only
had not been so frightened; generally, I have such a long
breath.' Then I praised her heartily and with the best
conscience in the world; for just that part with the long
G at the close she had done so well, taking the three
following and connecting notes in the same breath, as
one seldom hears it done; and therefore it amused me
doubly that she herself should have begun about it.

"After this Prince Albert sang the Arondte-lied, 'Es
Ist Ein Schmitter'; and then he said I must play him
something before I went, and gave me as themes the
chorale which he had played on the organ, and the song
he had just sung. If everything had gone as usual, I
ought to have improvised most dreadfully badly, for it
is almost always like that with me when I want it to go
well—and then I should have gone away vexed the whole
morning. But—just as if I was to keep nothing but the

pleasantest, most charming recollection of it—I never improvised better. I was in the best mood for it, and played a long time, and enjoyed it myself; so that between the two themes I brought in the two songs which the Queen had sung, naturally enough; and it went off so easily that I would gladly not have stopped; and they followed me with so much intelligence and attention that I felt more at ease than I ever did in improvising to an audience. She said several times she hoped I would soon come to England again, and pay them a visit; and then I took leave." The Queen, it may be added, always took a deep interest in Mendelssohn's work and career, and a marble bust of him has been placed by her command in the corridor at Windsor Castle.

A visit to Belgium and a meeting with some of the French Royal Family had been proposed for the Autumn of 1842, but the melancholy death of the Duke of Orleans, brother of the Queen of the Belgians, entirely disarranged all these plans, and a short tour in Scotland was arranged at the conclusion of the session. Parliament was prorogued by the Queen in person on the 12th of August. Her Majesty, in a speech, referred to the reverses sustained by the army of the westward of the Indus, and to the subsequent defense of Jellahabad, and, in touching on home affairs, which were in a dangerous condition, particularly at Manchester, where rioting had assumed formidable proportions, she said: "There are, I trust, indications of gradual recovery from that depression which has affected many branches of manufacturing industry, and has exposed large classes of my people to privation and sufferings, which have caused me the deepest concern. You will, I am confident, be actuated on your return to your several counties, by the same enlightened zeal for the public interests which you have manifested during the discharge of your Parliamentary duties; and will do your utmost to encourage by your example, and active exertions, that spirit of order and submission to the law which is essential to the public happiness, and without which there can be no enjoyment of the fruits of peaceful industry, and no advance in the career of social improvement."

On the 29th of August the Queen and Prince Albert, attended by the Duchess of Norfolk and Lord Morton, with other members of their households, embarked at Woolwich in the Royal George, commanded by Lord Adolphus Fitzclarence. The yacht, in tow of a steamer, was saluted on reaching Tilbury Fort, and passed along the coast, welcomed everywhere by demonstrations of loyalty. About one a. m., on the 1st of September, the royal squadron came to anchor in Aberlady Bay. Shortly after eight, Her Majesty landed at Granton pier, and proceeded at once to Dalkeith Palace, the home of the Duke of Buccleuch; escorted through Edinburgh by the Duke, and the Archers of the Royal Body Guard. On the 3d, the Queen made her public entry into the Scottish capital, escorted by the Inniskilling Dragoons. At the Canongate the Body Guard of Archers joined the procession, the 53rd Regiment guarding the line of route. At the barriers which had been erected near the Exchange, the Lord Provost, accompanied by the members of the Council, in their robes of office, presented the keys of the city, which were returned by Her Majesty with the words: "I return the keys of the city with perfect confidence into the safe keeping of the Lord Provost, Magistrates, and Council." At the Castle gate the Queen was received by Sir Niel Douglas, commanding the forces, and, alighting from the carriage, was conducted through the ancient fortress, where she inspected the various objects of interest, noticing particularly Mons Meg, and the ancient regalia of the Scottish Kingdom, deposited in the Crown Jewel Office. In her Journal the Queen writes: "The view from both batteries is splendid, like a panorama in extent. We saw from them Heriot's Hospital, a beautiful old building, built in the time of James by a jeweler, whom Sir Walter Scott has made famous in his 'Fortunes of Nigel." After this we again got into the carriages, and proceeded in the same way as before, the pressure of the crowd being really quite alarming. Both I and Albert were quite terrified for the Archer's Guard, who had very hard work of it; but they were of the greatest use. They all carry a bow in one hand, and have their arrows tuck through their belts. Unfortunately, as soon as we were out of Edinburgh, it began to rain, and continued raining the whole afternoon without interruption. We reached Dalmeny, Lord Rosebery's, at two o'clock. The park is beautiful, with the trees growing down to the sea."

On the 5th the Queen held a Drawing-room in the gallery of Dalkeith Palace. Holyrood House was not available for this State ceremony, on account of a dangerous fever lately prevalent in the vicinity. The Drawing-room was very numerously attended, and before it Her Majesty received and responded to addresses from the Lord Provost and the Magistrates, from the Scottish Church, and from the Universities of St. Andrew's, Glasgow and Edinburgh. On the 6th the Duke of Buccleuch's royal guests left Dalkeith, and, crossing from Queensferry into Fifeshire, proceeded to Dupplin Castle, where they lunched with the Earl of Kinnoull, on their way to Scone Palace, the seat of the Earl of Mansfield, where they dined and slept. Next morning, after inscribing their names in the Guildry books of the City of Perth, the last royal signatures in which were those of James VI. and Charles I., the Queen and Prince started for Taymouth, the seat of the Marquis of Breadalbane. On the 10th of September, after planting trees as a memorial of their visit, they left Taymouth, and were rowed for 16 miles up Loch Tay to Auchmore, whence they journeyed by Crieff to Drummond Castle, and there they were received by Lord and Lady Willoughby D'Eresby. Here, on the 12th, the Prince shot his first stag. On the 13th a visit was paid to Stirling, and, after a journey of 65 miles, Dalkeith was again reached. The last day of this visit, the first of many subsequently paid to the Northern Kingdom, was spent in seeing Roslyn Chapel and Hawthornden. Leaving Dalkeith, early on the morning of September the 15th, and embarking on board the Trident, a steamer belonging to the General Steam Navigation Company, the Queen and Prince reached Woolwich Dockyard on the morning of the 17th, and arrived at Windsor shortly after noon.

Writing on the next day to the Duchess of Saxe-Gotha, Prince Albert thus records his impressions of the country: "Scotland has made a most favourable impression upon us both. The country is full of beauty and of a severe and grand character; perfect for sport of all kinds, and the air remarkably pure and light in comparison with what we have here. The people are more natural, and marked by that honesty and sympathy which always distinguishes the inhabitants of mountainous countries, who live far away from towns. There is, moreover, no country where historical traditions are preserved with such fidelity, or to the same extent. Every spot is connected with some interesting historical fact, and with most of these Sir Walter Scott's accurate descriptions have made us familiar." Before quitting Scotland, the Queen had expressed her own gratification at the heartiness of her reception, in a letter to Lord Aberdeen: "The Queen cannot leave Scotland without a feeling of regret that hr visit on the present occasion could not be further prolonged. Her Majesty fully expected to witness the loyalty and attachment of her Scottish subjects; but the devotion and enthusiasm evinced in every quarter, and by all ranks, have produced an impression on the mind of Her Majesty which can never be effaced."

On the 10th of November, the Queen and Prince Albert, with the royal children, left Windsor for Walmer Castle, near Deal, the official residence of the Lord Warden of the Cinque Ports, which had been placed at their disposal by the Duke of Wellington. Here they were received by His Grace, and enjoyed the sea breezes till the 3rd of December. At all the places on their journey through Kent, particularly at Canterbury, the travelers were received with every demonstration of loyalty and affection.

On the 23rd of November, a special messenger from Downing Street brought dispatches containing the welcome news of the recapture of Ghuznee and Cabul, the defeat of Akbar Khan, and the liberation of his captives. On the same day the Queen heard, with much delight, of the Peace that had been concluded with China, on terms that afforded a new opening for commercial enterprise, and gave a fresh stimulus to the trade of the manufacturing districts, where want of employment had caused widespread suffering and discontent.

On the 2nd of February, 1843, Parliament assembled. For the first time since her accession, the Queen was unable to open it in person. On the 25th of April, Her Majesty's third child and second daughter was born at four a. m., Prince Albert and the Lord Steward, the Earl of Liverpool, being present. On the same day, at Pembroke Dockyard, took place the launch of Her Majesty's yacht the Victoria and Albert, which was then looked upon as one of the most beautiful steamers afloat, and has ever since been the favourite vessel of the Queen. The infant Princess was christened on the 2nd of June, in the Private Chapel at Buckingham Palace. The sponsors were the King of Hanover, represented by the Duke of Cambridge; the Hereditary Prince of Saxe-Coburg and Gotha, represented by the Hereditary Grand Duke of Mecklenburg-Strelitz; the Princess of Hohenlohe Langenburg, represented by the Duke of Kent, and the Princess Sophia Matilda of Gloucester. The rite was performed by the Archbishop of Canterbury, and the infant received the name of Alice Maud Mary.

On the 29th of June the Queen, accompanied by Prince Albert and the King and Queen of the Belgians, visited Westminster Hall to inspect the prize cartoons prepared for the decoration of the new Houses of aPrliament, which were then exhibited to the public. This exhibition was the result of the labours of the Royal Commission on the Fine Arts, of which the Prince was President. The execution of the cartoons in fresco has unfortunately not been successful; the artists were not familiar with the peculiar conditions of the technical process of the work, and little now remains to be seen of their designs. The Queen and the Prince showed their own personal interest in this little-practiced method of decoration by erecting a pavilion in the grounds of Buckingham Palace, the walls of which were covered with designs in fresco by Eastlake, Landseer, Maclise, Uwins, Leslie, Stanfield, and others. In a leter written at the time, Uwins remarks: "History, Literature, Science, and Art seem to have lent their stores to form the mind of the Prince. He is really an accomplished man, and, withal, possesses so much good sense and consideration, that, taken apart from his playfulness and good-humour, he might pass for an aged and experienced person, instead of a youth of two or three-and-twenty. The Queen, too, is full of intelligence, her observations very acute, and her judgment matured apparently beyond her age. * * * Coming to us twice a day, unannounced and without attendants, entirely stript of all state and ceremony, courting conversation, and desiring reason rather than obedience, they have gained our admiration and love. In many things they are an example to the age. They have breakfasted, heard morning prayers with the household in the private chapel, and are out some distance from the Palace talking to us in the summer-house before half-past nine o'clock — sometimes earlier. After the public duties of the day, and before their dinner, they come out again, evidently delighted to get away from the bustle of the world, to enjoy each other's society in the solitude of the garden."

Shortly after the cartoon exhibition, the Court removed to Windsor, where, on the 26th of August, the Queen, in honor of the Prince's twenty-fourth birthday, gave an entertainment at Virginia Water. Two days later, the Queen and Prince traveled to Southampton. There they met the new yacht, Victoria and Albert, which conveyed them to Cowes Roads. Next day they visited Norris Castle and Appuldurcombe, and, again embarking, proceeded

to Dartmouth, Plymouth, and Falmouth, where loyal addresses were presented. At Falmouth the Mayor, who
was a Quaker, was permitted to keep his hat on in the
royal presence. Thence the course was across the Channel to the coast of France.

The Queen had for some time been anxious to visit
Louise Philippe and to make the acquaintance of Marie
Amelie and their family, with whom the Queen had been
long connected by the marriage of her uncle, King Leopold, with the Princess Louise of Orleans. A favourable
opportunity now presented itself for a friendly visit, as
the French Court was at the Chateau d'Eu, near Treport. In Lord Bloomfield's Reminiscences occurs the
following story of an incident of the voyage: "I remained on deck a long time with Her Majesty, and she
taught me to plait paper for bonnets, which was a favourite occupation of the Queen. Lady Canning and I
had settled ourselves in a very sheltered place, protected
by the paddle-box; and, remarking what a comfortable
spot we had chosen, Her Majesty sent for her camp-stool,
and settled herself beside us, plaiting away most compos-
edly, when suddenly we observed a commotion among
the sailors, little knots of them talking together in a
mysterious manner; first one officer came up to them,
then another, looking embarrassed, and at that Lord
Adolphus Fitzclarence was called. The Queen, much
puzzled, asked what was the matter, and inquired whether we were going to have a mutiny on board? Lord
Adolphus laughed, but remarked that he really did not
know what would happen unless Her Majesty would be
graciously pleased to remove her seat. 'Move my seat,'
said the Queen, 'why should I? What possible harm can
I be doing here?' 'Well, ma'am,' said Lord Adolphus,

'the fact is Your Majesty is unwittingly closing up the door of the place where the grog tubs are kept, and so the men cannot have their grog.' 'Oh, very well,' said the Queen, 'I will move on condition that you bring me a glass of grog.' This was accordingly done, and after tasting it, the Queen said, 'I am afraid I can only make the same remark I did once before, that I think it would be very good if it were stronger.' This, of course, delighted the men, and the little incident caused much amusement on board."

When the royal yacht arrived at Treport, King Louis Philippe came off in his barge to welcome his guest. The Queen in her Journal writes: "I felt at it came nearer and nearer, more and more agitated. At length it came close, and contained the King, Aumale, Montpensier, Augustus (Prince of Saxe-Coburg and Gotha, and husband of Princess Clementine of Orleans), M. Guizot, Lord Cowley, and various officers and ministers. The good kind King was standing on the boat, and so impatient to get out that it was very difficult to prevent him, and to get him to wait till the boat was close enough. He got out and came up as quickly as possible and embraced me warmly. It was a fine and really affecting sight, and the emotion which it caused I shall never forget. The King expressed again and again how delighted he was to see me." As the Queen left her own yacht the Royal Standard was lowered from the masthead, and hoisted side by side with that of France on the King's barge. It was the first time they had floated together since the Field of the Cloth of Gold. On landing the Queen was escorted by the King up a somewhat steep stair to where the Queen Amelie with the Queen of the Belgians and other members of the Royal Family awaited their approach. After an interchange of cordial greetings and amid the firing of salutes and the shouts of the spectators, the royal cortege departed for the Chateau. In the evening a grand banquet was given. The Queen sat on the right of the King of the French, and on Her Majesty's right was the Prince de Joinville. Queen Amelie sat opposite the King, having Prince Albert on her right.

Next day, being Sunday, was spent very quietly; the Queen had no chaplain with her, but prayers were read by one of the members of the suite. "At half-past two," the Queen records in her Journal, "the King and Queen came to fetch us and took us over the greater part of the chateau. The number of family pictures is quite enormous. The little chapel is beautiful, and full of painted windows and statues of saints, etc., quite a little bijou. It is the first Catholic chapel I have seen. There are numbers of pictures and reminiscences of Mademoiselle de Montpensier. She built part of the chateau, and there are some interior decorations still of her time. The rooms of the Queen, including a little cabinet de toilette, are charming. They contain many old family pictures, and pictures of their own family, and there are some of poor Chartres, when a child, the sight of which, we see, is heartrending to the dear, excellent Queen."

On Monday, September the 4th, the Journal proceeds, "Up at half-past seven and breakfasted at eight. Good news from the children. The band of the 24th Regiment (Infanterie legere) played under my window, and extremely well. . . . At half-past ten the King and family came and fetched us to their delightful, cheerful breakfast. I sat between the King and Aumale. I feel so gay and happy with these dear people. . . . Later we saw M. Guizot, who came to express his great joy at our visit. It seems to have done the greatest good, and to have caused the greatest satisfaction to the French. . . . I hear that I should have been most kindly received at Paris even. The French naval officers give this evening a banquet on board the Pluton to our naval officers, and I trust that the 'haine pour les perfides Anglais' will cease."

The great event of the day was a fete champetre at the Mont d'Orleans in the forest of Eu. About four o'clock the King, with Queen Victoria and the Queen of the French, with other ladies, drove up to the large tent, which was pitched on a spot commanding the finest view, and here the party lunched. Prince Albert, with other gentlemen, had already arrived on horseback. The Queen records: "I sat between the King and Queen. Poor Helene (the widowed Duchess of Orleans) sat next the King; it was the first time she had sat at table with them since her terrible misfortune. . . . The King's liveliness and vivacity, and little impatiences, are my delight and amusement." After luncheon, the King, giving his arm to Queen Victoria, walked around the platform before the tent; Prince Albert came next, with the Queen of the French, the rest of the company following. The large crowd which had assembled cheered the Royal party with much enthusiasm. On the return to the chateau, after dinner, "There was," as the Queen notes, "very fine music by the artistes du Conservatoire. They played beautifully, particularly the things from Beethoven's symphonies."

The next morning Prince Albert, accompanied by the Dukes of Aumale and Montpensier and others, was present at a review of the French cavalry regiment, the Carabiniers, and afterwards of a regiment of the line, at the

Caserne de Montpensier. In the afternoon the whole party visited the church of Notre-Dame, and the crypt containing the monuments of the Counts of Artois and the Counts of Eu, the maternal ancestors of the King. On this day the King presented Queen Victoria with two splendid pieces of tapestry representing the chase of the Calydonian boar and the death of Meleager, which had been in hand at the Goeblins for thirty years and now form the principal decoration of Her Majesty's dining-room at Windsor.

The next day there was another fete champetre in the forest, the scene being the Mont St. Catherine, and the dejeuner entirely al fresco, no tent having been pitched. "We came home," the Queen writes—"the evening love-ly—at half past six. After dinner we remained in a little room near the dining-room—as the galerie where we generally are was fitted up as un petit theatre. At a little after nine we went in. The little stage and orchestra were perfectly arranged and we were all seatd in rows of chairs one above the other. The pieces were all admirably per-formed. The first was Le Chateau de Ma Niece, in which Madame Mira acted delightfully; the second, L'Humoriste, in which Arnol sent us into fits of laugh-ter. . . . Thursday, September 7. At a quarter to six we got up, le coeur gros at the though we must leave this dear interesting family. At half-past six the King (who, with all the Princes, was in uniform) and the Queen and all the family came to fetch us to breakfast. Join-ville was already gone to Treport. I felt so sad to go. At half-past seven we went in the large State carriage, pre-cisely as we came the day we arrived, with the Princes riding, and the same escort. It was a lovely morning and many people out. We embarked in the King's fine barge with great facility. . . . At last the mauvais moment arrived, and we were obliged to take leave and with great regret. . . . We stood on the side of the paddle-box, and waited to see them pass by in a small steamer, which they had all got into, and the King waved his hand and called out 'Adieu! Adieu!' We set off before nine. . . . At half-past three we got into the barge off Brighton, with Joinville, the ladies, Lord Aberdeen, and Mr. Tonchard. . . . When we arrived at the Pavilion, ew took Joinville up stairs with us, and he was very much struck with the strangeness of the building."

A few days after their return the Queen and Prince Albert again embarked on their yacht; and landed at Ostend to pay a visit to the King and Queen of the Belgians. They remained in Belgium for nearly a week, visiting Bruges, Ghent, Brussels, and Antwerp. To the Prince the old masters of the Low Countries were a great delight, and he afterwards formed the collection of their works since bequeathed to the National Gallery. After their return the Queen and Prince paid, in October, a visit to Cambridge, where, the next morning, the degree of LL. D. was conferred on the Prince. On the return journey to Windsor two days were spent at Wimpole, the seat of Lord Hardwicke.

Before the close of the year other visits were paid. One to Sir Robert Peel at Drayton Manor gave the Prince an opportunity long desired of inspecting some of the chief manufactories of Birmingham. Another was paid to Chatsworth, where three days were spent, and a third to Belvoir. Of the visit to Birmingham, the Prince writes to Baron Stockmar: "Sir James Graham and others had advised me strongly not to go, as the town is entirely in the hands of the Chartists, and even the Radicals dare not show themselves in it. Nevertheless I was received with an indescribable enthusiasm. The people regarded the visit as a great proof of confidence, and did all they could to give assurance of their loyalty. In short, our excursion was one unbroken triumph."

On the 29th of January, 1844, Prince Albert lost his father after a few days' illness. The sympathy of the Queen in his trial was one consolation. Writing to Baron Stockmar a few days afterwards, he mentions his sister-in-law Alexandrine as being, in the house of mourning at Coburg, "the consoling angel. Just such," he continues, "is Victoria to me, who feels and shares my grief, and is the treasure on which my whole existence rests. The relation in which we stand to one another leaves nothing to desire. It is a union of heart and soul." The Queen, too, had her trial to bear. When Easter came and Parliament adjourned, the Prince left England, feeling that duty demanded his presence in Coburg; since her marriage she had never been one day apart from him, and the separation was proportionately painful.

In June, 1844, shortly after the Prince's safe return, the Queen received a visit from the Emperor of Russia. The Emperor at first took up his quarters at the Russian Embassy, but afterwards, on Her Majesty's pressing invitation, became the Queen's guest at Buckingham Palace. The object of this visit he stated in one of his interviews with Sir Robert Peel: "Years ago Lord Durham was sent to me, a man full of prejudices against me. By merely coming to close quarters with me all his prejudices were driven clean out of him. This is what I hope by coming here to bring about with you, and with England generally. By personal intercourse I trust to annihilate these prejudices, for I esteem England highly; but as to what the French say about me I care not." The Queen, writing on the 11th of June to her uncle, thus records the personal impression made upon her by her visitor: "I will now give you my opinions and feelings on the subject, which I may say are Albert's also. I was extremely against the visit, fearing the gene and bustle, and even at first I did not feel at all to like it; but by living in the same house together quietly and unrestrainedly (and this Albert, and with great truth, says is the advantage of these visits, that I not only see these great people, but know them), I got to know the Emperor and he to know me. There is much about him which I cannot help liking, and I think his character is one which should be understood, and looked upon for once as it is. He is stern and severe, with strict principles of duty which nothing on earth will make him change. Politics and military concerns are the only things he takes great interest in; the arts and all softer occupations he does not care for; but he is sincere, I am certain—sincere even in his most despotic acts—from a sense that it is the only way to govern. . . . He was not only civil, but extremely kind to us both, and spoke in the highest praise of dearest Albert to Sir Robert Peel, saying he wished any Prince in Germany had as much ability and sense. He is not happy, and that melancholy which is visible in the countenance made us sad at times."

The hearty reception given to the Emperor by the Court, and by the whole nation, caused some irritation in the political circles of France. It even seemed at one time as if the projected visit of King Louis Philippe might be interfered with for this reason; and the Queen, in the letter to her uncle, an extract from which has been already quoted, writes: " I hope you will persuade the King to come all the same in September. Our motives and politics are not to be exclusive, but to be on good terms with all—and why should we not? We make no secret of it."

This irritation, and the estrangement between the two countries, were, however, intensified at this moment by the harsh measures adopted by the French officials to Queen Pomare in Tahiti. The extreme gravity of the situation caused much anxiety and suffering to our Queen, who was at the time in need of quiet and repose, as on the 6th of August her second son was born. In the first letter she was able to write after her confinement, she says to King Leopold: " The only thing almost to mar our happiness is the heavy and threatening cloud which hangs over our relations with France, and which, I assure you, distresses and alarms us sadly. The whole nation here is very angry. . . God grant all may come right, and I am still of good cheer." In September, when all disputes had been satisfactorily arranged, the Queen again wrote to her uncle: " The good ending of our difficulties with France is an immense blessing; but it is really and truly necessary that you and those in Paris should know that the danger was imminent. . . . We must try and prevent these difficulties for the future."

The infant Prince who had appeared at this critical moment was christened at Windsor on the 6th of September, 1843, receiving the names of Alfred Ernest Albert. At this ceremony the Prince of Prussia was present, afterwards the first Emperor of Germany and father-in-law of the Princess Royal. Three days later, the Queen and Prince with their eldest child left Windsor for Scotland. Landing at Dundee, they took up their residence at Blair Athol, which had been placed at their disposal by Lord Glenlyon, subsequently Duke of Athole. There they arrived on the 11th, and stayed till the end of the month, returning to Windsor, on the 3rd of October, to receive the King of the French. The King landed on the 8th at Portsmouth, where he was received by Prince Albert and the Duke of Wellington, who accompanied him to Windsor. The Queen in her Journal writes of her guest: "I never saw anybody more pleased or more amused in looking at every picture and bust. He knew every bust and everything about everybody here in a most wonderful way. Such a memory, such activity! . . . He is enchanted with the castle, and repeated to me again and again (as did also all his people) how delighted he was to be here, how he feared that what he had so earnestly wished since I came to the throne would not take place."

On the 9th of October the King was invested by Her Majesty with the Order of the Garter, an honor which had been conferred on His Majesty's predecessors, Charles X. and Louis XVIII., and in earlier years on Francis I., Henry II., and Charles IX. As the Queen, on her visit to France, had not entered Paris, it was not thought advisable that the King of the French should visit London. But on the 12th of October the King received an address from the Lord Mayor and Corporation of London, who came to Windsor in State for the purpose. The reply of the King to their address had a great effect on English feeling. "The union of France with England," he said, "is of great importance to both nations, but not from any wish of aggrandizement on the part of either. Our view should be peace, while we leave every other country in possession of those blessings which it has pleased Divine Providence to bestow upon them. France has nothing to ask of England, and England has nothing to ask of France, but cordial union."

Soon after the termination of the King's visit, on October 28th, the Queen opened the new Royal Exchange. The Queen, describing the ceremony to her uncle, writes: " I seldom remember being so pleased with any public show, and my bloved Albert was most enthusiastically received by the people. . . . The articles in the papers, too, are most kind and gratifying. They say no sovereign was ever more loved than I am (I am bold enough to say), and this because of our happy domestic home, and the good example it presents."

This feeling was not confined to London. Northampton, stronghold of Radicalism though it was, welcomed the Queen with loyal enthusiasm, when, during the next month, she passed through the city on the way to Burleigh. A similar welcome greeted her when, in the early part of the next year, 1845, she and the Prince paid visits, first to Stowe, the seat of the Duke of Buckingham, and afterwards to Strathfieldsaye, where the Duke of Wellington realized his cherished wish to entertain his Sovereign under his own roof. Of this visit Mr. Anson writes: "The Duke takes the Queen in to dinner, and sits by Her Majesty, and after dinner gets up and says, 'With your Majesty's permission I give the health of Her Majesty'; and then the same for the Prince. They then adjourn to the library, and the Duke sits on the sofa by the Queen for the rest of the evening, until eleven o'clock, the Prince and the gentlemen being scattered about in the library or the billiard room, which opens into it. In a large conservatory beyond, the band of the Duke's Grenadier regiment plays throughout the evening."

The Queen and Prince returned to Windsor on the 4th of February for the reassembling of Parliament, which was opened by Her Majesty in person. In the Royal speech, mention was made of the visits of the Emperor of Russia and the King of the French, and the more cordial relations established with the latter nation; the success of recent measures for supplying the deficiencies in the public revenue was noticed; the probable increase of the navy estimates owing to the progress of steam navigation was alluded to; and the policy of extending the facilities of academical education in Ireland was recommended. Notwithstanding the state of political tension, on the 6th of June the Queen gave her second costume ball at Buckingham Palace. The guests all wore the dress of the period of George II.; it was, to quote Greville, "most brilliant and amusing."

When the King of the French left England he was accompanied by the Queen and Prince Albert so far as Portsmouth. This gave them an opportunity of inspecting the estate of Osborne, which had been brought to their notice by Sir Robert Peel, who knew their wish to have a seaside residence more convenient and private than the obsolete Pavilion at Brighton. The inspection was satisfactory, and negotiations for the purchase of the estate were concluded in March, 1845. Adjoining land has since been added, so that the whole estate now extends over 2,000 acres. The old house not having sufficient accommodation for the Royal household, a new building was erected, the first stone of which was laid in the following June. The laying out and planting of the grounds, and the working of the home farm, were sources of endless delight to the Prince. Writing at the time to Baron Stockmar, he says: "Our property pleases us better and better every day, and is a most appropriate place of residence for us. It gives us the opportunity of inspecting the experimental squadron (which consists of five sail of the line, four frigates and several steam vessels), and of having it manoeuvred before us. Since the war no such fleet has been assembled on the English coast, and it has this additional interest, that every possible new invention and discovery in the naval department will be tried."

On the 9th of August, 1845, the Queen in person prorogued Parliament, and the same evening Her Majesty and the Prince started from Woolrich in the Royal Yacht for Antwerp, on their way to pay a visit to the King of Prussia, who met his Royal guests at Aix-la-Chapelle, and traveled with them to Cologne. From that city the Queen visited Bonn, where so much of Prince Albert's youth was spent. Thence they passed up the Rhine, and after spending one day at the King's Castle of Stotzenfels, on the 19th entered Coburg. Here they were reecived by the Duke Ernest, and by the King and Queen of the Belgians and the Duchess of Kent. During their stay at Coburg and Queen and Prince were lodged at the Rosenau, occupying the room in which the Prince had been born, and on the 26th keeping the Prince's birthday. On the next morning, "with heavy hearts," the Queen and he left the well-loved place for Rheinhardtsbrunn. This, next to the Rosenau, pleased the Queen more than any of the places she had visited, and here she would have gladly stayed longer; but time did not permit. After a few days' sojourn at Gotha, the journey homeward was continued by the Rhine to Antwerp, where the Victoria and Albert met the Royal party. The yacht left the Scheldt on the 7th of September, and next morning arrived off Treport, where the King and Queen of the French received them as their guests for one night at the Chateau d'Eu.

The winter of 1845-6 was an anxious and critical time. The appearance of the potato disease in Ireland seemed to foreshadow a famine, and the consequent necessity of a settlement of the Corn Law question agitated the whole of the political world. During the progress of the struggle between the rival parties the Queen, on the 25th of May, 1846, gave birth to her third daughter, who, on the 25th of July, was christened Helena Augusta Victoria, her sponsors being the Duchess of Orleans, represented by the Duchess of Kent, the Hereditary Grand Duke of Mecklenburg-Strelitz, and the Duchess of Cambridge.

The Court removed from Buckingham Palace to Osborne on the 7th of August, and on the 18th the Queen and Prince, with some of their children, started for a cruise in the Victoria and Albert. They visited Weymouth, Mount Edgcumbe, and the Channel Islands, with which they were much delighted. They also saw the Land's End and St. Michael's Mount, and landing at Fowey, inspected the Castle and Mine of Restormel. Returning to the Isle of Wight on the 10th of September, they took possession a few days later of their new home at Osborne. In the same autumn they stayed with Queen Adelaide at Cassiobury, and thence passed to Hatfield, where they met the Duke of Wellington, Lord John Russell, and Lord Melbourne, who, since his retirement from public life, had been very rarely seen by the Queen. Later in the year a visit was, paid by the Queen and

Prince to the Duke of Norfolk at Arundel. Christmas was spent at Osborne.

On February the 12th, 1847, the Chancellorship of the University of Cambridge became vacant by the death of the Duke of Northumberland, and on the 27th Prince Albert was elected to the vacant post, to the great gratification of the Queen, who, writing to her uncle, says: "Of course you have seen that Albert (after having declined, so that he had nothing to do with the unseemly contest) has been elected Chancellor of Cambridge. He could not do otherwise than accept it. We have been gratified at the great kindness and respect shown towards Albert by such numbers of distinguished people." The public installation of the Prince took place in July, when he was accompanied by the Queen to Cambridge, where they stayed at the Lodge of Trinity College. On the day of installation at the Senate House, the Queen was received at the door by the Prince and conducted by him to her place; then after the giving of the prizes, the Installation Ode, written for the occasion by Wordsworth, the Poet Laureate, was performed; concerts, receptions, and a levee were held, and after a most successful visit in beautiful weather, the Court returned to Buckingham Palace.

On the 23d of July the Queen in person prorogued Parliament in the recently-completed House of Lords, and on the 11th of August the Queen and Prince, who had gone from London to the Isle of Wight, left Osborne, with their two eldest children, on the Royal yacht for a journey to Scotland, where they proposed to stay at Ardverikie, a shooting lodge placed at their disposal by Lord Abercorn, who rented it from Lord Henry Bentinck. On the way the Scilly Isles were visited, then

Milford Haven and the Isle of Man, whence the squadron passed to the West Coast of Scotland, and up the Clyde to Dumbarton; and, passing the Kyles of Bute, up Loch Fyne to Inverary, where the Queen was received by the Duke and Duchess of Argyll in true Highland fashion. Here the Queen saw for the first time the young Marquis of Lorne, just two years old, afterwards to become her son-in-law. On leaving Inverary, Staffa and Iona were visited, and at Fort William Prince Albert went to Glencoe. From Fort William the whole party journeyed by land to Loch Laggan, by which Ardverikie is built. It was then remarkable for the drawings made on the walls by Sir E. Landseer, which unfortunately were destroyed later by fire. After a month's stay at this delightful spot, details of which are to be found in the Queen's "Leaves from the Journal of Our Life in the Highlands," the Royal party left for the south on the 17th of September, and landing at the new harbor of Fleetwood, after a short stay at the Isle of Man, returned to London.

Christmas was spent at Windsor, and with the new year came the beginning of the great outbreak of revolution which spread over all the Continent. Writing to Stockmar on the 27th of February, 1848, Prince Albert says: "The posture of affairs is bad; European war is at our doors; France is ablaze in every quarter; Louis Phillipe is wandering about in disguise; so is the Queen. . . . Guizot is a prisoner, the republic declared, the army ordered to the frontier, the incorporation of Belgium and the Rhenish provinces proclaimed. Here they refuse to pay the income tax, and attack the Ministry; Victoria will be confined in a few days; our poor good grandmamma (the Duchess Dowager of Gotha) is

taken from this world." The King and Queen of the
French eventually landed at Newhaven, and were joined
at Claremont by the other members of their family; here
they passed the remainder of their lives. Amid the gloom
of these events, a Princess was born at Buckingham Palace on the 18th of March, and was christened Louise
Caroline Alberta on the 14th of the following May by
the Archbishop of Canterbury.

Throughout these stormy and troublous times the
Queen continued in excellent health and spirits. Writing on the 4th of April to King Leopold, Her Majesty
says: "From the first I heard all that passed; and my
only thoughts and talk were politics. But I never was
calmer and quieter, or less nervous. Great events make
me calm; it is only trifles that irritate my nerves."

The leaders of the Chartist movement in London at
this time were endeavoring to imitate the revolutions in
Continental States. A huge demonstration was planned
for the 10th of April, 1848, when they announced their
intention to assemble on Kennington Common to the
number of 150,000, and to present to Parliament a mon-
ster petition, which, it was stated, had been signed by
more than 5,000,000 sympathizers. The magnitude of
the assembly, and the threats of their leaders, were met
by the Government with well-devised preparations. The
Bank and other public buildings were put in a state of defense, and more than 170,000 civilians enrolled themselves
as special constables, among the number being Prince
Louis Napoleon, afterwards Emperor. The Duke of
Wellington, as Commander-in-Chief, disposed the troops
at his command in readiness for any real disturbance,
should it arrive, and in conversation at Lord Palmerston's
house, said to Chevalier Bunsen: "Yes, we have taken

our measures; but not a soldier or piece of artillery shall you see, unless in actual need. Should the force of law, the mounted or unmounted police, be overpowered or in danger, then the troops shall advance—then is their time! But it is not fair on either side to call them in to do the work of police; the military must not be confounded with the police, nor merged in the police." Owing to the admirable precautions taken for the public safety, the demonstration was a complete and ignominious failure. The Queen and Prince, under the advice of the Ministry, had left London for Osborne, whence, on the following day the Queen addressed to the Duke of Wellington the autograph letter which has, by permission, been reproduced opposite page 104. In Ireland, at the same time, the forces of sedition were particularly active; but the timely arrest of the leaders, and the sentence of John Mitchell to transportation for fourteen years, effectually checked any serious insurrection.

On the 5th of September, 1848, when Her Majesty prorogued Parliament in person, she was able to say: "I have had the satisfaction of being able to preserve peace for my own dominions, and to maintain our domestic tranquility. The strength of our institutions has been tried, and has not been found wanting. I have studied to preserve the people committed to my charge in the enjoyment of that temperate freedom which they so justly value. My people, on their side, feel too sensibly the advantages of order and security, to allow the promoters of pillage and confusion any chance of success in their wicked designs."

On the 8th of the same month the Queen saw for the first time Balmoral, which had been rented from the Earl of Aberdeen on the recommendation of Sir James Clark.

The site and scenery delighted both the Queen and Prince, who soon became possessors of the whole domain, which they afterwards enlarged, till it has become one of the finest estates in the Highlands, and the Queen's favorite abode. In the Queen's "Leaves from the Journal of Our Life in the Highlands," she gives her impression of the place: "We walked out and went up to the top of the wooded hill opposite our windows, where there is a cairn, and up which there is a pretty winding path. The view from here, looking down upon the house, is charming. * * * It was so calm and so solitary, it did one good as one gazed around; and the pure mountain air was most refreshing. All seemed to breathe freedom and peace, and to make one forget the world and its sad turmoils. The scenery is wild, and yet not desolate; and everything looks much more prosperous and cultivated than at Laggan. Then the soil is delightfully dry. We walked beside the Dee, a beautiful, rapid stream which is close behind the house. The view of the hills towards Invercauld is exceedingly fine. In the first deer drive in the Balloch Buie forest, the Prince shot a fine royal stag; and the keepers said 'it was Her Majesty's coming out that brought good luck.' I was supposed to have a lucky foot, of which the Highlanders think a great deal."

Christmas of this year was spent at Windsor, and here, a few days later, was given the first of the series of theatrical performances which was continued at intervals till 1861. Her Majesty had always delighted in the dramatic art, and was a constant visitor to the theatres as well as the Opera in London, and the playbill of very performance she has honored with her presence has been carefully preserved. The performances at Windsor Castle took place during the stay of the Court in the Winter season, and were given in the large room on the north side known as the Rubens Room, in which a stage of fairly ample dimensions could be erected. The first performance was "The Merchant of Venice," in which Mr. and Mrs. Charles Kean appeared as Shylock and Portia. Mr. Kean continued to direct the entertainments till he gave up his London management in 1857, and under his direction thirty-five performances were given. After his retirement, Mr. W. B. Donne, Her Majesty's Examiner of Plays, was intrusted with the direction, and under him ten more evenings were devoted to dramatic representations. Plays of Shakespeare were performed on fourteen occasions. The last of this series of entertainments was on the 31st of July, 1861. The next Christmas was the time of the saddest sorrow in the life of the Queen, and it was not till thirty years had passed away that a stage was erected and that the Queen again witnessed a play in the Castle. In March, 1891, the Savoy Theatre Company performed "The Gondoliers." The stage was not as formerly in the Rubens Room, but was fitted up at one end of the Waterloo Gallery, which afforded more ample accommodation. Since then, at various times, other performances have taken place, and the Queen has had the opportunity of seeing the most eminent of the actors and actresses of the day. Besides these professional performances, the members of the Royal Family, many of whom have inherited the Queen's love of drama, have organized in the comparative privacy of Osborne and Balmoral, entertainments of a similar character, carried out with much care and completeness.

On the 2d of February, 1849, the Queen again personally opened Parliament. The outlook was clouded by

the continued distress in Ireland and by a revolt in the
Punjab; the latter was speedily quelled, but the former
still gave ground for serious anxiety. It had long been
the wish of the Queen and Prince to visit Ireland, and it
was hoped that the sympathy of their sovereign, marked
by her presence among her suffering subjects, might
have a cheering influence. In August, therefore, the
Queen and Prince, with their four children, embarked
at Cowes on the Royal yacht, under an escort of four
steamers, and landed at the Cove of Cork. At the moment when the Queen stepped for the first time on Irish
shore, the sun burst in splendor from the clouds, and to
a deputation of the townsmen Her Majesty communicated her pleasure that the town of Cove, in commemoration of her visit, should henceforth bear the name of
Queenstown. Having re-embarked, the Royal party proceeded up the river to Cork, where their reception was
most enthusiastic. The Queen in her Journal specially
notes, "The beauty of the women is very remarkable and
struck us much; such beautiful dark eyes and hair, and
such fine teeth; almost every thind woman was pretty,
and some remarkably so."

On the morning of August the 5th, the squadron
dropped down the river, and made direct for Dublin, arriving at Kingstown the next afternoon. Of this approach to the capital of Ireland the Queen says: "It is a
splendid harbor, and was full of ships of every kind. The
wharf, where the landing place was prepared, was densely crowded; and, altogether, it was a noble and stirring
scene. It was just seven when we entered, and the set-
ting sun lit up the country, the fine buildings, and the
whole scene with a glowing light, which was truly beautiful. We were soon surrounded by boats, and the en-

thusiasm and excitement of the people were extreme."
The Queen landed on 6th of August, and, passing
through Dublin to the Vice-Regal Lodge in the Phoenix
Park, was again highly gratified with her reception. "It
was," as she records in her Journal, "a wonderful and
striking scene, such masses of human beings, so enthusiastic, so excited, yet such perfect order maintained;
then the number of troops, the different bands stationed
at certain distances, the waving of hats and handker-
chiefs, the bursts of welcome which rent the air—all made
it a never-to-be-forgotten scene, when one reflected how
lately the country had been in open revolt and under mar-
tial law." On the 8th the Queen held a Court and Levee
at the Castle, at which addresses were received from the
Lord Mayor and Corporation, the University, the clergy,
and others, and two thousand of the Irish gentry were
presented. Next morning was devoted to a review, and
in the evening the Queen again visited the Castle to hold
a drawing-room, at which one thousand six hundred
ladies were presented. After a short visit to Carton, the
seat of the Duke of Leinster, Her Majesty re-embarked
at Kingstown. It is recorded that, as the yacht approached the end of the pier where the crowd was dens-
est, the Queen ran along the deck and, mounting the
paddle-box to join Prince Albert, took his arm, and
waved her hand to the people on the piers. The speed
of the vessel was slackened, and the Royal Standard was
lowered five times in courtesy to the cheering thousands
on shore.

After a rough passage Belfast was reached, where the
reception was as loyal and hearty as in Cork and Dublin. In her progress through the city Her Majesty witnessed with much interest the exhibition of the flax and

linen manufacture. In the afternoon the Royal party returned down the Lough, intending to make for the Firth of Clyde; but a heavy gale rendered it impossible to get under way, and it was not till the next afternoon (Sunday) that it was decided to attempt the journey. After a most tempestuous passage, Loch Ryan on the west coast of Argyllshire was reached, and the yacht anchored. From Loch Ryan Prince Albert made a visit to Loch Lomond, the weather being too stormy for the Queen to attempt to accompany him, and rejoined Her Majesty at Roseneath Bay, whence they proceeded to Glasgow, and after spending a night in Perth, passed by the Spittal of Glenshee to Balmoral, where their younger children were waiting their arrival.

The life of the Queen and the Prince in their Highland home is best described in the Queen's own book; but an interesting account of a visit paid to the Castle during this year (1849) is given by Greville in his Journal: "I am glad to have made this expedition, and to have seen the Queen and Prince in their Highland retreat, where they certainly appear to a great advantage. The place is very pretty, the house very small. They live here without any state whatever; they live not merely like private gentlefolk, but like very small gentlefolk—small house, small rooms, small establishment. There are no soldiers, and the whole guard of the Sovereign and the whole Royal Family is a single policeman, who walks about the grounds to keep off impertinent intruders or improper characters. . . . They live with the greatest simplicity and ease. The Prince shoots every morning, returns to luncheon, and then they walk and drive. The Queen is running in and out of the house all day long, and often goes about alone, walks into the cottages, and sits down and chats with the old women. I never before was in society with the Prince, or had any conversation with him. * * * I was greatly struck with him. I saw at once (what I had always heard) that he is very intelligent and highly cultivated, and, moreover, that he has a thoughtful mind, and thinks of subjects worth thinking about. He seemed very much at his ease, very gay, pleasant, and without the least stiffness or air of dignity."

The Prince's mind was indeed at this moment full of things worth thinking about. Before leaving London for the visit to Ireland he had held the first meeting on the subject of the Great Exhibition, which was two years later to inaugurate a new era in the arts and manufactures of the country. The first germ of the movement may be traced to the Frankfort fairs of the sixteenth century. The idea was still further devoleped by the French, who brought together great collections of art and industry with a view to the improvement of both. The Society of Arts in London had also held on a small scale several exhibitions of the same nature, which had produced beneficial results on our own manufactures. But to Prince Albert is due the idea that, by making this kind of exhibition international—an idea for the first time practicable owing to the improved means of communication afforded by steam and rail—an opportunity would be given for every country to show what it could produce in raw material and finish products of every kind, as well in the arts as in manufactures. This would enable each nation to see what itsel. was doing, and to compare its work with that of other countries whose competition in the markets of the world would have to be taken into account. On the 30th of July the Prince summoned to Buckingham Palace four of the most active members of the Society of Arts—Mr. Cubitt, Mr. Cole, Mr. Fuller and Mr. Scott Russell, and to them he explained his views. These gentlemen, with Mr. Digby Wyatt, undertook to make the necessary inquiries of the great body of manufacturers throughout the kingdom, and to see whether the idea would meet with their favor and support. Their reports proved highly encouraging. The sympathies of the Colonies and of the East India Company were enlisted, and the cordial assent of the Prince-President of the French Republic was given. From this time the movement went forward, without serious hindrance, towards the attainment of its magnificent success.

On the 27th of September the Queen and Prince left Balmoral, and, halting for a night at Howick on a visit to Earl Grey, proceeded to Osborne. There, a few days afterwards, news reached them of the sudden death of Mr. Anson, the Prince's private secretary, and Keeper of the Queen's Privy Purse—offices afterwards filled by Colonel the Hon. Sir Charles Phipps and General the Hon. Charles Grey. Of the Prince's regard for Mr. Anson mention has already been made.

The opening of the new Coal Exchange of the City of London had been fixed for the 30th of October, 1849, but the Queen was unfortunately prevented from performing the ceremony in person owing to a slight attack of chicken-pox. The building was therefore opened by Prince Albert, accompanied on the occasion by the Prince of Wales and the Princess Royal, who thus made their first public appearance. The route to the city was by water. The Royal barge, manned by seven-and-twenty watermen, conveyed the party down the river, which on the north side was covered by a line of steamers moored close to each other from Whitehall to London Bridge, and on the south side by a similar line of barges and lighters, the whole of which were thronged with spectators. The Royal barge was escorted by the clty barge, and followed by the barges of the Admiralty and the Trinity House. No pageant of the same character had been seen on these waters for scores of years, and has never been witnessed again. On landing at the Custom House, an address was presented to Prince Albert, after which the party were entertained at luncheon by the Lord Mayor, when, among other toasts, the health of the Prince of Wales and the Princess Royal was received with enthusiastic demonstrations.

For some time past the Dowager Queen Adelaide had been seriously ill, and on th 2d of December she died at her house at Stanmore. A few days before, the Queen and Prince Albert had seen her for the last time, and in a letter to King Leopold the Queen wrote: "I shall never forget the visit we paid to the Priory last Thursday. There was death written in that dear face. It was such a picture of misery, of complete aneantissement—and·yet she talked of everything. I could hardly command my feelings when I came in, and when I kissed twice that poor dear thin hand . . . I love her so dearly. She has ever been so maternal in her affection to me. She will find peace and a reward for her many sufferings." Again on the 4th the Queen wrote to her uncle: "Though we daily expected this sad event, yet it came as suddenly, when it did come, as if she had never been ill, and I can hardly realize the truth now. You know how very kind she was at all times to me, and how admirably she behaved from the time the King died. She was truly motherly in her kindness to us and to our children, and it always made her happy to be with us, and to see us! She is a great loss to us both, and an irreparable one to hundreds and hundreds. She is universally regretted, and the feeling shown is very gratifying. . . Poor mamma is very much cut up by this sad event, and to her the Queen is a very great and serious loss."

The early part of 1850 was entirely devoted by the Prince to the organization of the great enterprises he had undertaken for the next year. He had received warm encouragement from many and influential quarters, but there was an undercurrent of hostile criticism which occasioned him much anxiety. The first great public meeting on the subject of the Exhibition, held on the 21st of February, at Willis's Rooms, was a conspicuous success. But the strongest impetus to the movement was given by the Prince himself in his speech at the banquet held at the Mansion House on the 21st of March, when he explained to the Ambassadors of foreign States, to the Royal Commissioners for the Exhibition, and to the chief magistrates of more than two hundred towns, his conception of the scope and purpose of the proposed Exhibition. This memorable speech, too long to be quoted in these pages, but well worth perusal, was received with enthusiasm. and the congratulations which the Prince received assured him that his cherished scheme had taken a firm hold on the hearts of the people. The Queen was deeply touched by the warmth with which her husband's powers of mind and heart were received, and writing to her uncle a few days afterwards, says of the Prince: "People are much struck by his great power and energy; by the great self-denial and constant wish to work for others which are so striking in his character. But this is the happiest life. Pining for what one cannot have, and trying to run after what is pleasantest, invariably end in disappointment."

Of the great self-denial invariably shown by the Prince a conspicuous instance occurred almost immediately after these lines had been written by the Queen. The Duke of Wellington proposed that the Prince should succeed him in his office as Commander-in-Chief. This "tempting offer for a young man," as the Prince himself terms it, was fully discussed, and eventually refused, for reasons which the Prince embodied in a letter to the Duke. One paragraph of this letter is quoted here, as it explains the course of action which his Royal Highness had adopted when first he became the Consort of the Queen, and this he continued to pursue while his life was spared to Her Majesty and to the nation. "Whilst a female Sovereign has a great many disadvantages in comparison with a King, yet, if she is married, and her husband understands and does his duty, her position, on the other hand, has many compensating advantages, and, in the long run, will be found even to be stronger than that of a male Sovereign. But this requires that the husband should entirely sink his own individual existence in that of his wife; that he should aim at no power by himself or for himself; should shun all contention, assume no separate responsibility before the public, but make his position entirely a part of hers; fill up every gap which, as a woman, she would naturally leave in the exercise of her regal functions; continually and anxiously watch every part of the public business, in order to be able to advise and assist her at any moment in any of the multifarious and difficult questions or duties brought before her, sometimes international, sometimes political, or social, or personal. As the natural head of her family, superintendent of her household, manager of her private affairs, sole confidential adviser in politics, and only assistant in her communications with the officers of the Government, he is, besides, the husband of the Queen, the tutor of the Royal children, the private secretary of the Sovereign, and her permanent Minister." The Duke of Wellington was convinced by the arguments of the Prince, and Lord John Russell, to whom the whole correspondence, which may be found in Sir Theodore Martin's "Life," was submitted, also agreed in the conclusions at which the Queen and Prince had arrived.

On the 1st of May, 1850, the Queen's seventh child and third son was born at Buckingham Palace. The day was the birthday of the veteran Duke of Wellington, and this coincidence gave the Queen and Prince the opportunity of marking their friendship and esteem for one of their most valued subjects. Writing a few days afterwards to Baron Stockmar, the Prince says of the infant: "He is to be called Arthur William Patrick Albert. His first name is in compliment to the good old Duke, on whose eighty-first birthday he first saw the light. Patrick is in remembrance of our recent visit to Ireland; William, of the Prince of Prussia (late Emperor of Germany), whom we shall ask to be godfather, and also in remembrance of poor Queen Adelaide, on whose account we have also selected the Duchess Ida of Saxe-Weimar (Queen Adelaide's sister) as godmther. My name the Queen insists on retaining by way of coda." The infant Prince, now Duke of Connaught, was baptized in the following June, the Prince of Prussia and the Duke of Wellington both being present.

On the 27th of May the Queen was again the object of

a cowardly outrage while leaving Cambridge House, where her uncle was lying at the point of death. A man, dressed as a gentleman, darted forward and struck with a stick at the Queen's face; the force of the blow was fortunately broken by the bonnet, which was crushed in, but Her Majesty's forehead was severely bruised. The injury was not so serious as to prevent a visit to the opera in the evening, where, on the appearance of Her Majesty, the performance was stopped, and the National Anthem sung amidst enthusiastic cheering. The ruffian proved to be one Robert Pate, formerly holding a commission in the 10th Hussars. He was tried on the 11th of July, found guilty, and sentenced to seven years' transportation.

On the 29th of July of this year the Queen lost a valued friend and counsellor in Sir Robert Peel, who died from the effects of a fall from his horse on Constitution Hill. In a letter written to her uncle a few days afterwards, Her Majesty says: "The sorrow and grief at his death are most touching, and the country mourns over him as over a father. Every one seems to have lost a personal friend." Nor was this the only loss which this year was to bring. Before Sir Robert Peel was laid in his grave, the Duke of Cambridge, who had been long ill, died, and the news arrived of the serious illness of the Queen of the Belgians, an illness which proved fatal in October following. Her father, the exiled Louis Phillippe, had passed away at Claremont on the 25th of August, just as the Queen and Prince Albert were starting for Scotland to enjoy a brief respite from the cares of State, which, at this crisis, were more than usually burdensome, owing to the state of foreign affairs.

On the journey to the north the Queen and Prince

rested at Castle Howard, the seat of the Earl of Carlisle, and on the continuation of the journey to Edinburgh opened the railway bridge at Newcastle over the Tyne, and another at Berwick over the Tweed. At Edinburgh the Queen occupied the Royal palace of Holyrood, which then for the first time since the flight of Mary Queen of Scots sheltered a Queen. The stay in the northern capital was keenly enjoyed, the Queen especially admiring the view from Arthur's Seat, to which she climbed. During this visit the Prince laid the first stone of the Scottish National Gallery. The whole of the month of September was passed at Balmoral, and on the 10th of October the Royal party returned to the south, passing one night at Holyrood on the journey.

The serenity of the political atmosphere at the close of the year was seriously disturbed by a Brief from the Vatican, which re-established in the Kingdom of England a hierarchy of Bishops, deriving their tiles from English Sees. It came at a moment when the "Tractarian" movement had caused much excitement among the members of the Church of England, and the popular indignation at this "aggression" was raised to fervent heat. Sir Theodore Martin, in his Life of the Prince Consort, writes: "Men of all classes and all denominations poured in addresses to the Crown condemning in the strongest terms the invasion of the Royal supremacy, and urging determined resistance to the Papal pretensions. The Universities of Oxford and Cambridge, and the Corporation of London, sent their representatives by hundreds with similar addresses to Windsor Castle, where they were presented in St. George's Hall on the 10th of December. To each of these, replies were returned by Her Majesty in person. The Oxford address, presented by the

Duke of Wellington as Chancellor, was noted at the time
as having been read by him 'in his peculiar energetic
manner, with great vigor and animation.' The Cambridge address," the same chronicler states, "was read by
the Prince 'with great clearness and well-marked empha-
sis,' and responded to by Her Majesty 'with great delib-
eration and with decided accents.'" These addresses
and replies were drawn up with a moderation which
might well have been imitated by some of Her Majesty's
Ministers. In a letter on the subject to her aunt, the
Duchess of Gloucester, the Queen writes: "I would
never have consented to say anything which breathed a
spirit of intolerance. Sincerely Protestant as I always
have been and always shall be, and indignant as I am to
those who call themselves Protestant while they are, in
fact, quite the contrary, I must regret the unchristian
and intolerant spirit exhibited by many people at the
public meetings. I canot bear to hear the violent abuse
of the Catholic religion, which is so painful and so cruel
towards the many good and innocent Roman Catholics.
However, we must hope and trust this excitement will
cease, and that the wholesome effect of it upon our
Church will be lasting."

On the 4th of February, 1851, Parliament was opened
by Her Majesty in person. The Queen was loudly
cheered, the cheers being mingled with the cry of "No
Popery!" Fierce debates on the Ecclesiastical Titles Bill
followed; the Government was beaten, and resigned; but,
as Lord Stanley was not prepared to form a Government,
Lord John Russell and his colleagues resumed office. It
was not till the middle of the year that the excitement
caused by the explosion died away. During this anxious
time the Queen and Prince were much occupied with the

hard work and anxieties caused by the approach of the opening of the Great Exhibition. Croakers and prophets of evil were busy all around. Writing to the Dowager Duchess of Coburg, the Prince, a fortnight before the appointed day, says: "Just at present I am more dead than alive from overwork. The opponents of the Exhibition work with might and main, to throw all the women into panic and drive myself crazy. The strangers, they give out, are certain to commence a thorough revolution here, to murder Victoria and myself, and to proclaim the Red Republic in England; the plague is certain to ensue from the confluence of such vast multitudes, and to swallow up those whom the increased price of everything has not already swept away. For all this I am to be responsible, and against all this I have to make efficient provision."

The success of the Exhibition is a matter of history; no building like it had ever before been seen, and no such collection of arts and manufactures had ever been brought together. Of the opening ceremony the Queen gives her own impressions in her diary: "May 1.—The great event has taken place—a complete and beautiful triumph—a glorious and touching sight, one which I shall ever be proud of for my beloved Albert and my country.
. . .   Yes, it is a day which makes her heart swell with pride and glory and thankfulness! . . . The glimpse of the transept through the iron gates, the waving palms, flowers, statues, myriads of people filling the galleries and seats around, with the flourish of trumpets as we entered, gave us a sensation which I can never forget, and I felt much moved. . . . The sight as we came to the middle, where the steps and chair (which I did not sit on) were placed, with the beautiful crystal fountain just in front of it, was magical—so vast, so glori-

ous, so touching. One felt—as so many did whom I have since spoken to—filled with devotion—more so than by any service I have ever heard. The tremendous cheers, the joy expressed in every face, the immmensity of the building . . . the organ (with two hundred instruments and six hundred voices) which sounded like nothing, and my beloved husband, the author of this 'Peace Festival,' which united the industry of all nations of the earth—all this was moving, indeed, and it was, and is, a day to live forever. God bless my dearest Albert, God bless my dearest country, which has shown itself so great to-day! One felt so grateful to the great God, who seemed to pervade all and to bless all. The only event it in the slightest degree reminded one of was the Coronation, but this day's festival was a thousand times superior. In fact, it is unique, and can bear no comparison, from its peculiarity, beauty, and combination of such different and striking objects. . . . I must not omit to mention an interesting episode of this day, viz., the visit of the good old Duke on this his eighty-second birthday to his little godson, our dear little boy. He came to us both at five and gave him a golden cup and some toys which he had himself chosen, and Arthur gave him a nosegay. We dined en famille, and then went to the Covent Garden Opera. I was rather tired, but we were both so happy, so full of thankfulness! God is indeed our kind and merciful Father!"

On the 13th of June Her Majesty gave a State ball of great magnificence, at which all the company wore costumes of the time of the Restoration, and on the 9th of July the Queen and the Prince accepted the invitation of the Lord Mayor and the Corporation of London to an entertainment to celebrate the success of the Great Exhibition. The route lay through the City from Temple Bar; it was brilliantly illuminated, and the crowd in the streets enormous. The Guildhall was magnificently decorated and supper was served in the ancient crypt.

After a short stay at Osborne the Queen and Prince returned to London for the prorogation of Parliament on the 8th of August and for another visit to the exhibition. On the 29th they arrived at Balmoral, now the property of Her Majesty, to enjoy the rest and quiet so much needed after the strain and anxieties of the summer. The journey was for the first time made by the Great Northern Railway. It had been arranged that on the return journey a visit should be paid to Liverpool, now the first shipping port of the kingdom. After halting at Lancaster to see "Gaunt's embattled pile," the Royal party paid a visit to Croxteth, the seat of the Earl of Sefton, whence, next morning, passing through Konwsley, they reached Liverpool. Here the warmth of their reception was unchilled by the unusually inclement weather. Having viewed the docks, Her Majesty left Liverpool by canal for Worsley Hall, the seat of the Earl of Ellesmere. Thence she visited Manchester, where, in finer weather, she was received by enthusiastic multitudes. The great feature of the reception was the gathering of eighty thousand children of schools of all denominations, who were arranged in fourteen tiers of galleries around the Peel Park. Of this spectacle the Queen in her diary speaks as "A most extraordinary and totally unprecedented sight. . . . All the children sang 'God save the Queen' extremely well together, the director being placed on a very high stand, from which he could command the whole park. It was a very pleasant and interesting visit. We went through Manchester and had an opportunity of seeing the extraordinary number of warehouses and manufactories it contains, and how large it is."

Windsor was reached on the 11th of October. On the 14th the Queen paid her final visit to the Exhibition, which was formally closed on the morrow. Lord John Russell, writing to the Queen on the 17th, sums up its career and results in the following words: "The grandeur of the conception, the zeal, invention, and talent displayed in the execution, and the perfect order maintained from the first day to the last, have contributed together to give imperishable fame to Prince Albert. If to others much praise is due for their several parts in the work, it is to his energy and judgment that the world owes both the original design and the harmonious and rapid execution. Whatever may be done hereafter, no one can deprive the Prince of the glory of being the first to conceive and to carry into effect this beneficent design, nor will the Monarchy fail to participate in the advantage to be derived from this undertaking. No Republic of the Old or New World has done anything so splendid or so useful." In acknowledging this letter the Queen wrote: "We are both much pleased and touched at Lord John's kind and gratifying expressions relative to the success of the Great Exhibition, the closing of which we must much regret, as, indeed, all seem to do. Lord John is right in supposing it is particularly gratifying to her to see her beloved husband's name stand ever immortalized by the conception of the greatest triumph of Peace which the world has ever produced, and by the energy and perseverance with which he helped to carry it out. To feel this and to see this so universally acknowledged by a country, which we both daily feel more attached to and more proud of, is indeed a source of immense happiness and gratitude to the Queen. . . . The day of the closing of the Exhibition (which the Queen regretted much she could not witness) was the twelfth anniversary of her betrothal to the Prince, which is a curious coincidence."

In November of this year the Queen lost her only remaining uncle on her father's side, by the death of Ernest, Duke of Cumberland and King of Hanover. On the 2nd of December, 1851, occurred the coup d'etat of Louis Napoleon.

The year 1852 opened more cheerfully, with a revival of trade, an influx of gold from Australia causing a season of such unusual animation and gaiety, that King Leopold was afraid of the effects for his nephew and niece. To calm his apprehension the Queen wrote to him on the 1st of June: "Allow me just to say one word about the London season. The London season consists for us of two State balls and two concerts. We are hardly ever later than twelve o'clock at night, and our only dissipation is going three or four times a week to the play or opera, which is a great amusement and delassement to us both. As for going out, as people do here every night, to balls and parties, and to breakfasts and teas all day long besides, I am sure no one would stand it worse than I should. So you see, dearest uncle, that in fact the London season is nothing to us. The person who really is terribly fagged during the season with business and seeing people so constantly is Albert. This often makes me anxious and unhappy."

Parliament was prorogued, somewhat early, on the 1st

of July, by the Queen in person, and two days afterwards
the Court moved to Osborne. From this center several
plasant yachting trips were made. Dartmouth, Plymouth, and Mount Edgcumbe were visited, and in the
smaller yacht Fairy a cruise was made up the Tamar.
Tempestous weather prevented a projected trip to the
Channel Islands, but on the 10th of August it was found
practicable to cross the Scheldt, and to pay King Leopold a visit at Laeken. Here the Queen and Prince remained until the 14th, and then crossed to England, the
weather again being boisterous. On the 30th the Court
left Osborne for Balmoral, whence they returned to
Windsor on the 14th of October, passing through Edinburgh, Preston and Chester to Bangor, to see the new tu-
bular bridge built by Mr. Robert Stephenson over the
Menai Straits. During this sojourn at Balmoral the
news came to he Queen that a large fortune had been left
her by a Mr. oJhn Camden Nield. Writing to King Leopold, Her Majesty remarked, "It is astonishing, but it is
satisfactory to see that people have so much confidence
that it will not be thrown away. And so it certainly will
not be." A sadder message reached Balmoral a few days
after, when the great Duke of Wellington on the 14th
passed peacefully away at Walmer Castle. A report had
been received on the mornig of the 16th, but was not
generally believed, and it was not till the afternon when
Her Majesty, who was sketching at the Dhu Loch, received a letter from Lord Derby, "which," the Queen
writes, "I tore open; and alas! it contained the confirmation of the fatal news that England's, or rather Britain's,
pride, her glory, her hero, the greatest man she had ever
produced, was no more! Sad day! Great and irreparable national loss! * * * In him centered almost ev-

ery earthly honour a subject could possess. His position
was the highest a subject ever had—above party, looked
up to by all, revered by the whole nation, the friend of
the Sovereign; and how simply he carried these hon-
ours! *   *   *   He was a link which connected us with
bygone times, with the last century. Not an eye will be
dry in the whole country." Immediately on her return
from Balmoral, the Queen issued a general order to the
army which the deceased soldier had so long commanded. Its closing paragraph ran as follows: "The discipline which he exacted from others, as the main foundation of the military character, he sternly imposed upon
himself; and the Queen desires to impress upon the army
that the greatest commander whom England ever saw
has left an example for the imitation of every soldier, in
taking as his guiding principle in every relation of life
an energetic and unhesitating obedience to the call of
duty." The public funeral of the Duke was celebrated
at St. Paul's on the 18th of November with great magnificence and solemnity.

On the 1st of December of this year the Senate and the
Legislative Corps of the French Republic announced to
their President that he had been elected Emperor of
France by a majority of seven millions and a half of votes.
Under the title of Napoleon III., the new Emperor was
recognized in England and by the principal foreign powers, with the exception of Russia.

On the 7th of April, 1853, the fourth son of Her Majesty was born at Buckingham Palace. The infant Prince
was christened at the same place on the 28th of June by
the Archbishop of Canterbury, receiving the names of
Leopold George Duncan Albert; the first after the King
of the Belgians, the second after his sponsor, the new

King of Hanover, and the third as a compliment to Scotland.

At this time the urgent representations of the Queen and the Prince had called the attention of the Ministry to the condition of our naval and military forces. In the early part of the year 1853 Chobham Common was selected for a camp to test the efficiency of the military organization. The idea of a permanent camp of instruction was also pressed upon the Government, and later on resulted in the acquisition of the tract of land where the military station of Aldershot is now fixed.

In the summer the site selected at Chobham was occupied by an encampment of a small, but well-appointed force of about 10,000 men of various branches of the service. The spectacle was novel and interesting to a generation which had not for nearly forty years had the opportunity of seeing a mass of troops together under arms. On the 21st of June the Queen and Prince Albert, with whom were the King of Hanover and the Duke of Coburg, witnessed the first trial of field manoeuvres. Her Majesty, mounted on a black charger, wore a military habit. An attack of measles, which ran through the whole family with the exception of the two youngest children, prevented the Prince from taking the active part in the work of the camp to which he had been looking forward to with eagerness; and it was not till the 4th of August that he was able to accompany the Queen to witness the operations, which were on that day carried out by the fresh body of troops which had taken the places of the original occupants of the camp. On the 6th they returned to Chobham with their four eldest children, celebrating by this treat the birthday of the Prince.

Of this visit the Queen wrote to King Leopold: "We went twice more to our dear (as I call it) camp, and had two interesting days there. It had been most successful, and the troops have been particularly well all the time. When I think that this camp, and all our large fleet, are, without doubt, the result of Albert's assidious and unceasing representations to the late and present government, without which I fully believe very little would have been done, one may be proud and thankful; but, as usual, he is so modest that he allows no praise. He works for the general good, and is sufficiently rewarded when he sees this carried out."

The camp was broken up on the 20th, having proved a complete success, and a most important and valuable training for the active warfare in which the troops which had taken part in it were soon to be engaged. The review of the large fleet assembled at Spithead took place on the 11th of August; the force assembled was the most powerful which, up to that time, had ever been brought together, consisting of six ships of the line propelled by steam, three sailing ships of the line, and sixteen steam frigates and sloops, carrying 1,076 guns and nearly 10,-000 men. The steam power, it was recorded with admiration at the time, was nominally of 9,680 horses, but really of double the amount, and therefore exceeded the horse-power of the whole collected cavalry of the State! The review had a melancholy interest also; it was the last time when a squadron of sailing ships of the line were watched from the English shores.

On the 29th of the same month the Queen, accompanied by Prince Albert and their two eldest sons, arrived at Kingstown from Holyhead to pay their long-expected visit to the Exhibition of Irish Industry, which had been opened earlier in the year at Dublin. They were received by the Lord Lieutenant and proceeded to the Viceregal Lodge, and on the following day visited the Exhibition. The Queen says of it, "Everything was well conducted, and the people most kind." In deplorable weather the Queen and Prince paid a visit the same day to Mr. Dargan, at whose sole expense the Exhibition building had been constructed. His demeanour is noted as "trustingly simple and modest. I would have made him a Baronet, but he was anxious it should not be done." After a week's stay in Dublin, during which every mornig was devoted to the Exhibition, the Royal visitors left Ireland on the 3rd of September. Writing on that date Her Majesty says: "A beautiful morning, and this the very day we are going away, which we felt quite sorry to do, having spent such a pleasant, gay, and interesting time in Ireland. * * * We drove quietly, though not at a foot's pace, through Dublin, which was unusually crowded (no soldiers lining the streets), to the station, where again there were great crowds. In eight minutes we were at Kingstown, where again the crowds were immense, and most enthusiastic. The evening was beautiful, and the sight a very fine one—all the ships and yachts decked out and firing salutes, and thousands on the quay cheering." On the following morning they crossed to Holyhead, and journeyed by rail to Balmoral. Here on the 28th the foundation-stone of the new house was laid with much ceremony.

It was in the early part of this year that the Prince had commenced a work which was a source of keen enjoy ment to him for the rest of his life, and helped to distract his mind from the worry and turmoil of foreign politics. With the Queen he had been paying much attention not only to the literary treasures with which, under the care of Mr. Glover, the new Royal Library was being gradually filled; he had also carefully examined, and superintended the rearrangement of, the great mass of drawings and engravings by old masters, left by George III., to which was added the priceless collection of portrait miniatures collected from the different palaces. Every evening, when time could be spared, the Queen and Prince would visit the Library, and spend hours in arranging these treasures, and here the Prince conceived the idea of illustrating the life and work of one great master—Raphael—by a complete series of reproductions of his designs, arranged systematically, with fac-similes of every known study for, and variation of, each subject. The acquisition of the early engravings and of the photographs necessary for a complete elucidation of the master's work in painting fresco or tapestry, was a matter of long and arduous labor, but the Prince lived to see a great mass of the work completed, and the catalogue of the collection, which has since been printed, remains as a lasting record of his power of organization, and a work of permanent interest to every student of art.

CHAPTER SEVEN.

In the winter of 1853 and the early part of the next year the Queen had much trouble to endure. War had been declared between Russia and Turkey, and public feeling in England, already vehemently excited, was raised to a supreme pitch by the destruction of the Turkish fleet at Sinope.

The resignation of Lord Palmerston, who represented the warlike spirit of the people, inflamed the public mind; a loud outcry was raised in the Press about Court intrigues, and absurd rumours were circulated that Prince Albert was acting as a hostile influence behind the throne. It was impossible for the Queen not to feel very keenly the injustice of these unfounded and mischievous attacks. In a letter to Lord Aberdeen of the 4th of January, 1854, she wrote: "In attacking the Prince, who is one and the same with the Queen herself, the throne is assailed; and, she must say, she little expected that any portion of her subjects would thus requite the unceasing labours of the Prince." On the 30th of January Parliament was opened by the Queen in person; the calumnies were completely refuted by the Ministerial leaders in both Houses, and the resolutions accorded to the Queen and the Prince is described by Her Majesty as "very friendly." In the course of the same letter, to Baron

Stockmar, she writes: "We are both well, and I am sure will now recover our necessary strength and equanimity to meet the great difficulties and trials which are before us."

These difficulties and trials were the most serious with which, since her accession, the Queen had been called upon to cope. For the first time she had been obliged to commence hostilities against one of the European Powers, and, as was stated in Her Majesty's declaration on the 28th of March, 1854, actuated "by a desire to divert from her dominions most disastrous consequences, and to save Europe from the predominance of a Power which had violated the faith of treaties, and defied the opinion of the civilized world, to take up arms, in conjunction with the Emperor of the French, for the defense of the Sultan. Her Majesty is persuaded that in so acting she will have the support of her people; and that the pretext of zeal for the Christian religion will be used in vain to cover an aggression undertaken in disregard of its holy precepts and of its pure and beneficent spirit." Before this formal declaration troops had already been despatched to the East. Of one detachment, the Queen in a letter to King Leopold, on February 28th, says:—"The last battalion of the Guards (Scots Fusileers) embarked to-day. They passed through the court-yard here at seven o'clock this morning. We stood on the balcony to see them. The morning fine, the sun shining over the towers of Westminster Abbey,and an immense crowd collected to see the fine men, and cheering them immensely as with difficulty they marched along. They formed line, presented arms, and then cheered us very heartily, and went off cheering. It was a touching and beautiful sight. Many sorrowing friends were there, and one saw the shake of many a hand. My best wishes and prayers will be with them all."

On the 10th of March the Court left London for the Isle of Wight. At Spithead lay the magnificent fleet, under the command of Sir Charles Napier, which was under orders to sail for the Baltic. Through the twenty ships, all but three propelled by steam, the Queen and Prince were conveyed in the Fairy from Portsmouth to Osborne. The next day, in the same yacht, they returned to witness the departure of the first division of the squadron for the North. The Fairy led for some miles, and then stopped while the fleet passed by, saluting as it went. The Queen, in a letter to Baron Stockmar, expresses her own feeling in these words: "I am very enthusiastic about my dear Army and Navy, and wish I had two sons in both now. I know I shall suffer much when I hear of losses among them."

During the progress of the War the thoughts of the Queen and Prince never strayed from the sailors and soldiers; the success of their arms was a source of deep pride and joy, but these feelings were saddened by the tales of loss, suffering, famine, and disease, which arrived from the Camp before Sebastopol. The winter was one of unusual severity, and the hardships caused by its rigour at home increased the sympathy felt by all classes, as each mail brought news of the sufferings of the troops on the bleak hills of the Crimea. To Lord Ragan at the close of the year the Queen wrote: "The sad privations of the Army, the bad weather, and the constant sickness are causes of the deepest concern and anxiety to the Queen and the Prince. The braver her noble troops are, the more patiently and heroically they bear all their trials and sufferings, the more miserable we feel at this long continuance. The Queen trusts that Lord Raglan will be very strict in seeing that no unnecessary privations are incurred by any negligence of those whose duty it is to watch over their wants. * * * Lord Raglan cannot think how much we suffer for the Army, and how painfully anxious we are to know that their privations are decreasing. * * * The Queen cannot conclude without wishing Lord Raglan and the whole of the Army, in the Prince's name, and her own, a happy and glorious New Year."

In the summer of 1854 the Queen and Prince received a visit from their young relatives, the King of Portugal and his brother the Duke of Oporto, the sons of the late Queen Donna Maria de Gloria, whom Her Majesty had known from her childhood. With the Queen and Prince they went to Ascot Races, and were present at the opening of the new Crystal Palace at Sydenham. On the 4th of September, in response to a very cordial invitation from the Emperor Napoleon, Prince Albert left Osborne for Boulogne, to inspect the encampments of French troops which had been formed in the vicinity. In the mutual liking and esteem which resulted from this visit began a lasting friendship, drawn closer by the tie of common sorrow which still unites the widowed Queen and the widowed and now childless Empress of the French.

Parliament, which had been opened by the Queen in person on the 12th of December, after a short but stormy and exciting session, in which the conduct of the Ministry was severely criticised, adjourned till the 23rd of January, 1855, when it re-assembled. The attacks on the Ministry were pressed with such energy, that Lord Aberdeen and his colleagues were forced to retire. Though the Queen's difficulties and anxieties were at length some-

what alleviated by the formation of a Ministry under
Lord Palmerston, yet the criticism of public men grew
more and more bitter. There was little brightness in the
position of things; the brilliant victories of Alma and
Inkermann had produced no tangible result; Sebastopol
still defied, and under Todleben grew stronger to defy,
the attacks of a force which, exposed to the rigour of a
Scythian winter, was daily thinned by sickness and privation.

On the 2nd of March, 1855, the Emperor Nicholas died
at St. Petersburg, and was succeeded by the Emperor
Alexander II. A week later began the series of delibera-
tions between the Powers of Europe for the restoration
of peace, which resulted in the abortive labour of the
Vienna conference. It was on the day following the receipt in England of the news of the death of the Czar,
that the Queen with the Prince visited the military hospitals at Chatham, where the wounded soldiers, who had
been conveyed home, were lying. The visit made a great
impression upon Her Majesty, who urged upon the Secretary of War the necessity for more military hospitals,
and for better arrangements for the treatment of their
inmates. The great establishmnt at Netley was the result of the direct intervention of the Sovereign.

On the 16th of April, 1855, occurred the memorable
visit of the Emperor Napoleon with the Empress to these
shores, an event remarkable from the fact that it arose
out of an alliance so unforseen that the whole tradition-
ary policy of Europe was based upon the assumption of
its impossibility. The succes of the visit was, however,
great and enduring. The Imperial visitors, after an enthusiastic welcome in the course of their journey from
Dover through London, arrived at Windsor Castle in the

evening, where they were received by the Queen and the Royal Family, and lodged in the principal suite of rooms on the north side, which had been before, by a strange irony of fate, tenanted by the Emperor Nicholas and by King Louis Philippe. The pleasing impression made upon the Queen by her first conversation with the Emperor was confirmed during the course of the visit. Her Majesty notes that her guest was "very quiet and amiable and easy to get on with. . . . Nothing can be more civil or amiable or more well-bred than the Emperor's manner—so full of tact." On the afternoon of the 17th a review was held in the Great Park, where the Queen, accompanied by the Empress, the Emperor and Prince Albert being on horseback, reviewed a body of cavalry, composed of the 2nd Life Guards, the Royal Horse Guards, the Carabaniers, and a troop of Horse Artillery, under the command of Lord Cardigan. In the evening there was a ball in the Waterloo Gallery, of which the Queen writes: "How strange to think that I, the grand-daughter of George III., should dance with the Emperor Napoleon, nephew of England's greatest enemy, now my nearest and most intimate ally, in the Waterloo Room, and this ally only six years ago living in this country an exile, poor and unthought of." "Strange indeed!" writes Sir Theodore Martin, "and none could have been so deeply impressed by the contrast as the Emperor himself, whn he looked round at the portraits, with which the room is paneled, of the great statesmen and soldiers, the struggle and glory of whose lives it had been to hold his famous ancestor in check." A view of this historic room is given opposite page 136.

Another ceremony, which must have called up strange thoughts in the minds of the spectators, took place next day, when at the Chapter of the Order of the Garter, held in the Throne Room, the Sovereign invested the Emperor with the Insignia of the Order. The last knight who had been invested by the Sovereign in person, in a full Chapter of the Order at Windsor, was King Louis Philippe. On the following day the Queen with her Imperial guests and the whole Court moved to Buckingham Palace, whence the Emperor and Empress paid a visit to the City of London, and in the evening, with the Queen and Prince Albert, to the Royal Italian Opera. The reception of the Imperial visitors on these occasions showed how cordially the alliance between the two Powers was welcomed by all classes of their subjects. The welcome was no less apparent the following day when the newly opened Crystal Palace at Sydenham was visited. The next day the Emperor and Empress took leave of the Queen, and escorted by Prince Albert as far as Dover, returned to France.

Of the visit the Queen has noted in her Journal: "It went off so well—not a hitch or contretemps—fine weather, everything smiling; the nation enthusiastic, and happy in the firm and intimate alliance and union of two great countries, whose enmity would be fatal. We have war now, certainly, but war which does not threaten our shores, our homes, and internal prosperity, which war with France must ever do. . . . I am glad to have known this extraordinary man. . . . I believe him to be capable of kindness, affection, friendship and gratitude. I feel confidence in him as regards the future." That the esteem was mutual may be inferred from an extract from the leter written to the Queen by the Em-

peror on the 25th of April, in which he says: "I feel it
to be my first duty to again assure you how deep is the
impression left upon my mind by the reception, so full of
grace and affectionate kindness, vouchsafed to me by
your Majesty. Political interests first brought us into
contact, but to-day, permitted as I have been, to become
personally known to your Majesty, it is a living and respectful sympathy by which I am, and shall be henceforth, bound to your Majesty. In truth, it is impossible
to live for a few days as an inmate of your home without yielding to the charm inseparable from the spectacle
of the grandeur and the happiness of the most united of
families. Your Majesty has also touched me to the heart
by the delicacy of the consideration shown to the Empress; for nothing pleases more than to see the person
one loves become the object of such flattering attentions."

On the 18th of May, 1855, in the centre of the Horse
Guards Parade, the Queen with her own hand presented
to the officers of the Army of the Crimea, and to a portion of the non-commissioned officers and privates of
regiments which had been engaged in the East, who had
returned to this country on leave, or disabled by
their wounds, the war medals they had deserved by their
gallant service. The Queen herself best describes this
touching ceremonial in a letter of the 22nd of May to the
King of the Belgians: "Ernest will have told you what
a beautiful and touching sight and ceremony (the first of
the kind ever witnessed in England) the distribution of
the medals was. From the highest Prince of the blood
to the lowest private, all received the same distinction
for the bravest conduct in the severest actions, and the
rough hand of the brave and honest private soldier came

for the first time in contact with that of their Sovereign and their Queen. Noble fellows! I own I feel as if they were my own children—my heart beats for them as for my nearest and dearest! They were so touched, so pleased—many, I hear, cried; and they won't hear of giving up their medals to have their names engraved upon them, for fear that they should not receive the identical one put into their hands by me! Several came by in a sadly mutilated state. None created more interest or is more gallant than young Sir Thomas Trowbridge, who had at Inkermann one leg and the foot of another carried away by a round shot, and continued comanding his battery till the battle was over. * * * He was dragged by in a Bath-chair, and when I gave him his medal I told him I should make him one of my aides-de-camp for his very gallant conduct, to which he replied, 'I am amply repaid for everything.' One must love and revere such soldiers as those."

On the 18th of August, 1855, the Queen and Prince Albert, accompanied by the Prince of Wales and the Princess Royal, left Osborne for Boulogne and Paris, to return the visit of the Emperor and Empress of the French to England. No English Sovereign had visited the French capital since the coronation of the infant Henry VI. at Paris in 1422. In 1688, James II., it is true, had sought the protection of Louis XIV., and was lodged by him in one of his palaces, but he was a fugitive and an exile, and the throne of England was occupied by his son-in-law. In 1815, four centuries after the expulsion of the Plantagenets, the generals of an English army, which had given the first Emperor Napoleon his final overthrow, and stormed the defenses of Paris, occupied its gates and palaces as conquerors. They restored to his throne the heir of the Bourbons, Louis XVIII., whose great-grandfather had waged war against England for the restoration of the heir of the Stuarts. Fifteen years later his brother, Charles X., fled again to England, and the throne of France was occupied by a Bourbon of the House of Orleans. He, in turn, eighteen years afterwards, fled to the shores of England, and there remained the guest of the English Queen. His fallen sceptre was seized by the nephew of the great Emperor whom the English arms had overthrown in 1814, and who had died a prisoner on an English island. The new ruler had lived in exile under the protection of the English laws; he had borne himself as a citizen of the land of his refuge, and, when the safety of its capital was menaced, had enrolled himself as a special constable for its defense. He was now absolute Sovereign of the French people, and the visit of the Queen of England to the French Emperor in his own capital was, therefore, from every point of view, a most remarkable event.

The Queen and Prince on their arrival passed through Paris to St. Cloud, which had been placed at their disposal by the Emperor, and here they were received by the Empress. The next day being Sunday was kept as a day of rest, and on Monday the Royal party, under the guidance of Prince Napoleon, inspected the Palais des Beaux-Arts, a portion of the Great Exposition de l'Industrie. On Tuesday a visit was paid to Versailles, and the next day was devoted to a further examination of the Palais de l'Industrie. On Thursday the Queen and Prince were conducted over the Louvre, with its multifarious treasures of art, and in the evning the Municipality of Paris gave a magnificent ball in the Hotel de Ville, which had been decorated with a brilliance and splendour surpassing all previous experience. On Friday, after again visiting the Palais de l'Industrie, the Queen was present at a review of forty-five thousand troops in the Champ de Mars, and exceedingly admired the appearance and equipment of the battalions. After this, as the Queen wrote in her Journal, "We drove straight to the Hotel des Invalides, under the dome of which Napoleon lies, late as it was, because we were most anxious not to miss this, perhaps the most important act of all in this very interesting and eventful time. It was nearly seven when we arrived. All the Invalides—chiefly of the former, but some of the present, war—were drawn up on either side of the court into which we drove. * * * There were four torches which lit us along, and added to the solemnity of the scene, which was striking in every way. The church is fine and lofty. We went to look from above into the open vault * * * the coffin is not yet there, but in a small side chapel de St. Jerome. Into this the Emperor led me, and there I stood, at the arm of Napoleon III., his nephew, before the coffin of England's bitterest foe; I, the grand-daughter of that King who hated him most and most vigorously opposed him, and this very nephew, who bears his name, being my nearest and dearest ally! The organ of the church was playing 'God Save the Queen' at the time, and this solemn scene took place by torchlight, and during a thunder-storm. Strange and wonderful indeed! It seems as if in this tribute of respect to a departed and dead foe, old enmities and rivalries were wiped out, and the seal of Heaven placed upon that bond of unity which is now happily established between two great and powerful nations. May Heaven bless and prosper it!"

On Saturday the Royal party visited the Palace of St.

Germains, where James II. of England lived and died in exile. In the evening the Emperor gave a splendid fete at Versailles, which outdid even the magnificence of the Hotel de Ville. Of this ball the Queen remarks: "It was one of the finest and most magnificent sights we had ever witnessed; there had not been a ball at Versailles since the time of Louis XVI., and the present one had been arranged after a print of a fete given by Louis XV." Sunday was again passed in quiet, and on Monday the homeward journey began. Boulogne was reached in the afternoon, and after a short rest, "We drove down," writes the Queen, "at once to the sands, where were assembled all the troops of the camp, thirty-six thousand infantry, besides cavalry, lancers, and dragoons, and the gendarmerie. We drove down the lines, which were immensely deep—quite a forst of bayonets. The effect they produced, with the background of the calm blue sea, and the seting sun, which threw a glorious crimson light over all—for it was six o'clock—was most magnificent. * * * Near the end of the march past our squadron saluted; and, indeed, is was one of the not least remarkable of the many striking events and contrasts with former times which took place during this visit, that at this very place, on these very sands, Napoleon I. reviewed his army which was to invade England, Nelson's fleet lying where our squadron lay, watching that very army. Now our squadron saluted Napoleon III. while his army was filing past the Queen of England, several of the bands playing 'Rule Britannia.' * * * We thanked the Emperor much for all his kindness and for this delightful visit. * * * It was past twelve when the Emperor left. * * * I shall always lookon this visit not only on account of the delightful and splendid things we saw and enjoyed, but on the time we passed with the Emperor, as one of the pleasantest and most interesting periods of my life. The Empress, too, has a great charm, and we are all very fond of her."

On the following morning, the Queen and Prince reached Osborne, and on the 7th of September, being, as the Prince wrote, "sorely in want of the moral rest and the bodily exercise," arrived at Balmoral, where the prinpal part of the new house was ready for their reception. Here in close succession came telegrams conveying the welcome news from the seat of war, of the sinking of the Russian ships in the harbour, of the capture of the Malakoff by the French, and, finally, that Sebastopol was in the hands of the Allies. On the receipt of this welcome news the Queen writes: "God be praised for it! Our delight was great; but we could hardly believe the good news, and from having so long, so anxiously expected it, one could not realise the actual fact. Albert said they should go at once and light the bonfire which had been prepared when the false report of the fall of the town arrived last year, and had remained ever since waiting to be lit. On the 5th of November, the day of the battle of Inkermann, the wind upset it, strange to say; and now again, most strangely, it only seemed to wait for our return to be lit. The new house seems to be lucky indeed, for from the first moment of our arrival we have had good news."

Another piece of good news, though of a different character, came to the Queen and Prince a few days later—best described by an extract from the Queen's "Leaves from the Journal": "September 29, 1855. Our dear Victoria was this day engaged to Prince Frederick William of Prussia, who had been on a visit to us since the 14th. He had already spoken to us on the 20th of his wishes; but we were uncertain, on account of her extreme youth, whether he should speak to her himself, or wait till he came back again. However, we felt it was better he should do so; and during our ride up Crag-na-Ban this afternoon he picked a piece of white heather (the emblem of good luck), which he gave to her, and this enabled him to make an allusion to his hopes and wishes, as they rode down Glen Girnoch, which led to this happy conclusion."

On the 2nd of January, 1856, the Queen opened Parliament in person with the usual ceremonial. The Speech from the Throne, after mentioning the signal and important successes of the Allies, continued: "The naval and military preparations for the ensuing year have necessarily occupied my serious attention; but while determined to omit no effort which could give vigour to the operations of the war, I have deemed it my duty not to decline any overtures which might reasonably afford a prospect of a safe and honourable peace. * * * Negotiations for such a treaty will shortly be opened at Paris."

On the 30th of March, 1856, at ten o'clock at night, the metropolis was aroused by the sound of a royal salute from St. James's Park, announcing the signature of the Treaty of Peace, which next day was officially proclaimed, to the joy and relief of the nation. The public celebration of the national rejoicing took place on the 29th of May, when the whole of London was brilliantly illuminated, and there were magnificent displays of fireworks from Hyde Park, the Green Park, Victoria Park, and Primrose Hill.

The news of the conclusion of an armistice had reached the Russian and the Allied Generals on the 28th of February, and the final evacuation of the Crimea took place on the 12th of July, when General Codrington formally gave up to the Russians Sebastopol and Balaclava.

On the 20th of March the Princess Royal was confirmed in the private chapel of Windsor Castle, her parents, her godfather the King of the Belgians, most of the members of the Royal Family, the great officers of State, and the members of the household being present. The Archbishop of Canterbury and the Bishop of Oxford took part in the ceremony.

On the 16th of April Her Majesty paid a second visit to the wounded soldiers at Brompton Hospitals. About four hundred convalescent patients were drawn up in the barrack square and in the hospital; all who were able to leave their beds were assembled, and received from the Queen, whom they had so gallantly served, kind words and marks of interest more precious even than the liberal donations which were left for the aleviation of their sufferings. Two days afterwards the Queen and Prince made a formal visit to Aldershot Camp, the arangements of which were now considered as completed. Alighting at Farnborough Station, Her Majesty was received by General Knollys, the Commandant, with his Staff. On arriving at the Camp the Queen exchanged her carriage for a chestnut charger, on which she rode to inspect the troops. These amounted in number to about 14,000 men, among them being several fine regiments of militia. The Queen with the Prince and the Royal Family remained in the camp the same night, and on the following morning witnessed a field-day, in which 18,000 troops took part. Her Majesty wore a Field Marshal's uniform, with the star and riband of the Garter, a dark blue skirt and scarlet tunic.

On the 23rd of the same month Spithead was the scene of a review by the Queen of the greatest naval force which up to that time had ever been assembled. Twenty-two steamships-of-the-line, of from 60 to 131 guns, 53 frigates and corvettes, 140 gunboats, 4 floating batteries, and 50 mortar vessels and mortar boats, composed this magnificent fleet, the number of the guns being 3,002, and the engines working to an aggregate power of 30,671. The Queen's yacht, steaming through the fleet, which was anchored in a double line, was saluted by each ship. The gunboats then steamed down the line, passing in review before Her Majesty; after which the Royal yacht anchored off the Nab Light, and was followed by the ships of the fleet under steam, who, passing round two pivots, returned in the same order to their former stations. These manoeuvres were executed with splendid accuracy and precision in a sea crowded with every kind of craft, and thronged to the utmost limits of their capacity by enthusiastic spectators. After dark, on a calm, still night, the whole fleet was illuminated; the lines of the masts and yards were traced out with lamps, and blue lights burned at every port.

On the 19th of May, 1856, the Queen crossed from Osborne to Netley, to lay the foundation-stone of the great Military Hospital. Writing next day to her uncle, Her Majesty says:—"Last week, but particularly on Sunday, it blew a fearful gale, and, if it had not moderated, we could not have performed the interesting ceremony of laying the first stone of a large Military Hospital, near Netley, the first of the kind in this country, and which is to bear my name, and be one of the finest in Europe. Loving my dear brave Army as I do, and having seen so many of my poor sick and wonuded soldiers, I shall watch over this work with maternal anxiety."

By the beginning of July the greater part of the British troops had returned from the Crimea. A field-day and review of those who were in camp at Aldershot had been arranged for the 8th, but was greatly marred by inclement weather. At the close of the usual evolutions the Crimean regiments advanced and formed three sides of a square round the Royal carriage. The officers who had been under fire, together with four men of each company and troop, stepped forward. The Queen's carriage was thrown open, and, rising from her seat, Her Majesty spoke to them as follows:—"Officers, non-commissioned officers, and soldiers! I wish personally to convey through you to the regiments assembled here this day my hearty welcome on their return to England in health and full efficiency. Say to them, that I have watched anxiously over the difficulties and hardships which they have so nobly borne, that I have mourned with deep sorrow for the brave men who have fallen in their country's cause, and that I have felt proud of that valour which, with their gallant allies, they have displayed on every field. I thank God that your dangers are over, while the glory of your deeds remains; but I know that should your services be again required, you will be animated with the same devotion which in the Crimea has rendered you invincible." The Queen's words were received with an outburst of cheering and waving of helmets, bearskins, and sabres. Next day London welcomed the Guards on their return home. The battalions marched from Vauxhall, by the Houses of Parliament, past Buckingham

Palace, from the centre balcony of which they were seen by the Queen as they went by Constitution Hill to Hyde Park. Here they were met by the Prince, who was soon joined by Her Majesty, and in brilliant weather four battalions of household and three of Crimean troops passed before their Sovereign—the closing scene of a long and arduous war.

The Court remained at Osborne till the 27th of August the Queen and Prince making occasional excursions by sea, among others one to Devon port, when the weather was so stormy that they were obliged to leave the yacht and return to Osborne by land. On the 30th Balmoral was reached, where the old house had now entirely disappeared. Here, as all over the kingdom, the weather continued cold, wet and stormy. Among the visitors at Balmoral, not the least honoured was Miss Florence Nightingale. On the 21st of September she was introduced to the Queen and Prince by Sir James Clark, with whom she was then staying at Birkhall. "She put before us," the Prince notes in his diary, "all tne defects of our present military hospital system, and the reforms which are needed. We are much pleased with her; she is extremely modest." A fortnight afterwards Miss Nightingale was invited to Balmoral, the time of her visit being fixed to coincide with that of Lord Panmure, the Minister for War, so that he might have the opportunity of hearing from her own lips the story of what she had seen, and the conclusions she had drawn from her great and remarkable experience in the East.

On the 16th of October the Court arrived at Windsor from Balmoral. From the begining of the next month the Queen heard the sad news that her half-brother, Prince Leiningen, had had a second stroke of paralysis;

from this he never recovered, and died at Wald-Lemin-
gen on the 13th. The Queen felt her loss most keenly.
Writing to her uncle on the 19th she says: "Oh, dearest
uncle, this blow is a heavy one—my grief very bitter. I
loved my dearest only brother most tenderly. You loved
him, you knew how delightful a companion he was.
. . . Mamma is terribly distressed, but calm and resigned, tnd thinks that God has taken our poor, dear
Charles in love and mercy to save him from more suffering." Again, a fortnight later, Her Majesty writes: "I feel
my loss very much. A sad, sad feeling comes over me
just when I may seem happiest and most cheerful. We
three were particularly fond of each other, and never felt
or fancied that we were not real geschwister (children of
the same parents). We knew but one parent, our mother, so we became very closely united, and so I grew up;
the distance which difference of age placed between us
entirely vanished. . . . God's will be done. November has brought us another sad anniversary."

The close of the year witnessed an event of no little
interest. During the last English Arctic Expedition one
of Her Majesty's ships, the Resolute, had been abandoned in the ice. Sixteen months afterwards she was discovered by some American explorers and taken by them
to America. There the derelict was refitted at the nation expense, and was sent to England by Congress as a
present to the Queen. On the arrival of the vessel Her
Majesty at once arranged to accept this gracious gift in
person, and on the 16th of December proceeded on board
for the purpose. The prompt and cordial courtesy of the
Sovereign produced a great effect upon the Americans,
who, as Lord Clarendon reported, "are most grateful to
your Majesty, and, as Mr. Dallas (the American Minis-

ter) says, are overwhelmed with the kindness of their reception here." The formal surrender of the ship to the British Government took place on the 30th, when, after the last gun of the salute from the Victory had been fired, the American flag was lowered, and the Union Jack floated again at the peak.

The year 1857, which was to end in such anxiety, opened in what seemed to be a prosperous and tranquil state. Europe was peaceful, and only in Persia and China was the nation in a state of hostility. On the 14th of April the Queen's youngest child was born, and two days after, the Queen heard with much grief of the sudden illness of her aunt, the Duchess of Gloucester, the last survivor of the family of George III. This most excellent and lovable Princess died, at the age of eighty-one, on the 30th of the month. Of her the Queen writes, in a letter to King Leopold: "Her age and her being a link with bygone times and generations, as well as her great kindness, amability and unselfishness, rendered her more and more dear and precious to us all, and we all looked upon her as a sort of grandmother. Her end was most peaceful." To her memory the Queen has since erected an alabaster tomb in the south aisle of St. George's Chapel in Windsor Castle, where she is buried.

The month of May was memorable for the opening of the marvelous Art Treasures Exhibition at Manchester, a collection of works of art of every kind and description, but more particularly of pictures of all schools, the like of which has hardly ever been brought together. The exhibition afforded a remarkable proof of a fact which before was not generally appreciated, namely, the enormous amount of works of art of the highest class gathered in the private collections throughout this country.

On the 19th of May the official announcement was made to Parliament, in a message from the Queen, of the intended marriage of the Princess Royal to Prince Frederick William of Prussia. The approval of the union by the representatives of the nation was manifested by the almost unanimous vote of the House of Comons to settle a dowry of £40,000, with an annuity of £4,000, upon the Princess Royal. A few weeks afterwards the Princess's youngest sister was christened in the private chapel at Buckingham Palace, receiving the names of Beatrice, Mary Victoria Feodora, the second of which was given in memory of the late Duchess of Gloucester.

On the 25th of June an order of Council was issued, conferring by letters patent the title and dignity of Prince Consort upon His Royal Highness Prince Albert. Hitherto the husband of the Queen had possessed no distinctive title, and no other place in Court ceremonial than that which he held by courtesy. This anomaly was now rectified. On the next day a ceremony of great interest took place in Hyde Park; this was the distribution to the gallant men who had earned it of the new decoration of the Victoria Cross. Up to this date there had been no badge or mark of distinction peculiarly destined to mark heroic deeds. Her Majesty, therefore, by Royal warrant, instituted a new naval and military decoration, to be designated "The Victoria Cross," bearing the inscription "For Valour," to be given only to men who, serving before the enemy, have performed some signal act of bravery or devotion to their country. Some time necessarily elapsed before the list of those entitled to this honour could be drawn up, and in order to inaugurate the institution of the order with becoming ceremony, Her Majesty resolved to confer the decoration upon its recipients in person. About 4,000 troops were drawn up in the Park, and more than 100,000 spectators assembled to witness the ceremony; the recipients of the Cross were sixty-two. Her Majesty, wearing a scarlet jacket with a black habit, and mounted on a grey roan, rode to the centre of the ground and pinned the Cross with her own hands upon the breast of each man as he was called up in turn. After all the brave warriors had received their decorations, Her Majesty reviewed the troops. On the 29th, the Queen and Prince, with their four eldest children, and Prince Frederick William of Prussia, left London, in order to inspect the Art Treasures Exhibition at Manchester, which the Queen had not been able to visit earlier in the year.

Towards the end of the month news arrived in England of the mutiny of the native regiments at Meerut on the 10th of May, and of the massacre by them of numbers of English officers, women and children, followed by the retreat of the mutineers to Delhi, and the spread of mutiny among the troops there. For some time past the disaffection among the native troops had been known, and some regiments disbanded; but the receipt of the news of the outbreak showed that a danger had arisen which imperilled the lives of thousands of English men, women and children, and menaced the very existence of the British Empire in the East. The Queen was especially grieved that, owing to a mistaken economy, the army at home had been reduced in number, and wrote to Lord Panmure very seriously on the subject, concluding with the words, "If we had not reduced in such a hurry this spring, we should now have all the men wanted."

The Queen and Prince spent the 17th and 18th of July at Aldershot in order to witness the evolutions of the troops there assembled under General Knollys. Five regiments of cavalry and ten battalions of infantry with a large force of artillery and engineers were engageα. Her Majesty watched the movements of the troops on horseback, wearing her usual military dress. A picture of the scene, painted by G. H. Thomas, is reproduced opposite page 144 by permission. In a memorandum sent by the Queen for communication to the Government on the measures to be taken to render her army able to cope with the demands made upon it by the increase of the Empire, and the pressing emergency of the Indian Mutiny, the concluding paragraph is as follows: "The present po- has just seen, in the camp at Aldershot, regiments which, sition of the Queen's army is a pitiable one. The Queen has just seen, in the camp at Aldershot, regiments which after eighteen years' foreign service, in most trying climates, had come back to England to be sent out after seven months to the Crimea. Having passed through this destructive campaign, they have not been home for a year before they are to go to India for perhaps twenty years. This is most cruel and unfair to the gallant men who devote their services to the country, and the Government is in duty and humanity bound to alleviate their position." Fortunately the heroic defenders of the Empire in India had not to wait for the reinforcements from home. The English regiments which had been despatched for the operations in China were, at the request of Lord Canning, the Governor-General, directed by Lord Elgin to be turned aside to Calcutta. Their arrival had an immediate influence in crushing the rebellion.

It was not only the total absence in the army of any reserve which could be of use on emergency which caused the Queen anxiety. On the 19th of August the Royal yacht, with the Queen and Prince and six of the Royal children on board, entered the harbour of Cherbourg. The visit was unexpected, and, after a stay of a couple of days, was brought to a close, the Victoria and Albert conveying Her Majesty to Alderney. Of this visit the Prince writes to Baron Stockmar: "We made a delightful run to Cherbourg and Alderney. Cherbourg is a gigantic work that gives one grave cause for reflection. The works at Alderney, by way of counter-defence, look childish." The Queen's own comment was, "It makes me unhappy to see what is done here, and how well protected the works are, for the forts and the breakwater (which is treble the size of the Plymouth one) are extremely well defended." What they had seen caused the Queen to call for reports on the progress that had been made with the works of defence at Portsmouth and elsewhere, as it was felt to be of the utmost importance that a sudden descent upon our shores should not find the country defenceless.

On the 29th of August, 1857, the Court arrived at Balmoral, where the details awaited them of the tragedy of Cawnpore. Delhi was uncaptured, Lucknow unrelieved. A special day of fast and humiliation was ordered, which was kept on the 7th of October throughout the country with great solemnity. On the 11th of October the Court returned to Windsor, having passed, on the way, a night at Haddo House, on a long-promised visit to Lord Aberdeen. From India news arrived of the capture of Delhi, and the victorious career of General Havelock.

This cheering intelligence was saddened by a private sorrow. The Duchess of Nemours, first cousin to the Queen and the Prince Consort, who had given birth to a daughter on the 28th of October, died suddenly, on No-

vember 10th, at Claremont. In a letter to Baron Stockmar the Prince writes: "The fresh disaster to which
eventful November has given rise in eventful Claremont
will have caused you deep emotion. I thought at once of
you and of the old wounds which the similarity of the
circumstances would re-open in your heart, just forty
years and four days since poor uncle lost his darling wife
in child-bed. Nemours has lost his dear, to us all so
dear, Victorie! in the room nearly above that in which the
Princess Charlotte died."

On Monday, the 25th of January, 1858, the Princess
Royal was married at St. James's to Prince Frederick
William of Prussia. The first marriage in the new generation was made the occasion of much rejoicing and
festivity in the metropolis. Four State representations
were given at Her Majesty's Theatre; a State Ball was
also held at Buckingham Palace. Of the ceremony itself
the Queen has recorded in her Diary: "The sun was
shining brightly; thousands had been out since very early, shouting, bells ringing, etc. Albert and uncle, in
Field-Marshal's uniform, with batons, and the two eldest
boys went first. Then the three girls in pink satin, trimmed with Newport lace, Alice with a wreath and the two
others with only bouquets in their hair of cornflowers
and marguerites; next the four boys in Highland dress.
* * * Then the procession was formed, just as at
my marriage, mama last before me—then Lord Palmerston with the sword of State, then Bertie and Alfred. I
with the two little boys on either side (which they say had
a most touching effect) and the three girls behind." This
extract exactly describes the group, reproduced opposite
page 152, from the picture by John Philip, R.A., of the
marriage ceremony. When this was over, the newly-

married couple drove down from St. James's to Buckingham Palace, whence they proceeded to Windsor, to
which two days afterwards the Court removed, and on
the following day the bridegroom was invested with the
Order of the Garter. On the 2nd of February came the
parting, the bitterness of which not even the thought of
the brilliant future, which lay before the Princes, could
soften.

Striking proof was given, at the beginning of the year
1858, that the apprehension of the Queen and Prince as
to the state of the army and the national defences, and
the want of preparation against sudden danger were not
groundless. Ten days before the Royal wedding occurred the attempt by Orsini and others to assassinate the
Emperor of the French. The plot, prepared by them in
England, was executed on the evening of January 14th,
as the Emperor and Empress arrived in their carriage at
the Opera House. Though the intended victims escaped
almost uninjured, ten of the surrounding crowd were
killed and one hundred and fifty-six wounded. The violent language, used in France against this country, not
only provoked extreme indignation on this side of the
Channel, but led to the subsequent formation of the great
Volunteer force, which now is looked upon as a valuable
and necessary addition to the forces of the Crown for the
purpose of national defence.

On the 2nd of August, 1859, the Queen bestowed the
Victoria Cross on twelve men who had won the distinction, some in the Crimea, some in India, and on the same
day was published the Act for the transfer of the Government of India to Her Majesty from the old East India
Company.

Two days later, the Queen and Prince Consort, with the Prince of Wales, embarked at Osborne to visit in state the great arsenal at Cherbourg, which they had seen privately the year before. The reception to the Royal visitors, given, as it was, at the very height of the friendship between the sovereigns, was, if noise constitutes welcome, hearty indeed. Never, in time of peace, had such a cannonade been heard.

Returning to England, the Queen and Prince Consort embarked, a few days later, for another visit to the Condemonstrative. Questions of reform at home, and danger of war between France and Austria on the question tinent, this time as the guests of their daughter in her own home. At Magdeburg they were met by Prince Frederick William, who escorted them to Wildpark Station, where the Princess Royal met her mother for the first time since her marriage. This happy visit lasted till August 27th, and on the 31st the Queen and Prince reached Portsmouth, to learn that Prince Alfred had just passed an excellent examination for the Navy.

On their way to Scotland, on the 6th of September, the Queen and Prince stopped at Leeds, a city which no British sovereign had ever before visited, and opened the New Town Hall—a building second only to St. George's Hall at Liverpool in size and beauty. The reception accorded them was enthusiastic in the extreme. From Balmoral the Court moved, on the 19th of October, to Windsor, where another gap in the family circle was created by the departure of Prince Alfred to join the Euryalus, which was attached to the Mediterranean fleet for two years.

The first month of the year 1859 brought with it one piece of good news, to mitigate the anxiety caused by the

critical condition of affairs on the Continent. This was
the birth of the first child of the Princess Frederick William, the Queen thus becoming a grandmother at the age
of forty. "The joy and interest taken here," the Queen
writes from England to King Leopold, "are as great as
in Prussia, which is very gratifying."

On the 3rd of February, 1859, Her Majesty opened
Parliament in person, and her reception was, owing to
the excited state of public feeling, unusually cordial and
of the possession of Lombardy, were the principal causes
of disquietude. By the beginning of May all hope of avert-
ing war, though it had not been officially declared, was
abandoned; and the struggle which was to end in such
momentous consequences to Italy had begun. A disso-
lution of Parliament had just taken place, followed by
a general election, and on the 7th of June Her Majesty
opened her new Parliament. In the House of Lords the
address was carried without a division, but in the House
of Commons an amendment, expressive of want of confidence, was carried, and on the resignation of Lord Derby, Lord Palmerston was entrusted with the formation of
the Ministry. The prorogation on the 13th of August
set the Queen and Prince free to seek fresh air and rest
in a short excursion to the Channel Islands, followed by
their departure for the Highlands. On the 14th of October, their journey south was interrupted in order that
the Queen might open at Loch atrine the waterworks
by which the town of Glasgow was supplied. On the
same journey a visit was paid to Penrhyn Castle, near
Bangor, where the famous slate quarries were inspected,
and the singing of the workmen was much admired. The
Princess Royal arrived with her husband from Berlin in
time for the Prince of Wales's birthday, on the 9th of

November; they stayed till the 3rd of the following month, to the great delight of their parents. Christmas was spent at Windsor.

"We began 1860 very peaceably and happily," the Queen writes, on the 3rd of January, to King Leopold, "and I never remember spending a pleasanter New Year's Day, surrounded by our children and dear mama." The Queen again opened Parliament on the 24th of January, and was accompanied for the first time by the Princesses Alice and Helena. In the early part of the year year was published the first series of the Idylls of the King, afterwards dedicated to the memory of Prince Albert. Though the aspect of affairs at home was bright, the Italian policy of the French Emperor and his dsigns upon Savoy were disquieting. His continued restlessness, the large additions to his army, and the great increase to his fleet, alarmed the country. In response to these threatening demonstrations, the inadequacy of the national defences, and the plans for necessary measures to be taken, were subjects of prolonged debate in Parliament. At the same time, the enthusiasm of the nation, now thoroughly aroused to its danger, caused an enormous increase in the number and efficiency of the Volunteer force. Of these citizens soldiers the Queen held a great review in Hyde Park on the 23d of June, when 21,000 men passed before Her Majesty. Later in the year, on the way to Balmoral, the Queen at Edinburgh inspected the Scottish volunteers, of whom 18,000 marched past in review order beneath Arthur's Seat. Of the whole force the Prince, who took the warmest interest in the movement, writes: "The Volunteers have already run up to 124,000 men, and make an excellent appearance—a proof there is no lack of patriotism in the country." On the 2d of July the Queen, who had become Patron of the National Rifle Association, opened its first meeting at Wimbledon, and fired the first shot at a target on this historic ground, and made the first bull's-eye ever scored upon its targets. The Queen's Prize has always been the blue ribbon of the annual competition.

In June, 1860, the Prince, writing to Baron Stockmar, announced a piece of news of much family interest: "The two young Princes of Hesse-Darmstadt leave England to-day, and have just taken leave. There is no doubt that the eldest (Louis) and Alice have formed a mutual liking, and although the visit fortunately has passed over without any declaration, I have no doubt that it will lead to further advances from the young gentleman's family. We should not be averse to such an alliance, as the family is good and estimable, and the young man is unexceptionable in morals, manly, and both in body and mind distinguished by youthful freshness and vigor. As heir-presumptive to the Grand Duchy his position would, moreover, not be unsuitable. . . . The Queen and myself look on as passive observers, which is undoubtedly our best course, as matters at present stand." A month later the Princess Charles of Hesse, mother of Prince Louis, informed the Princess Frederick William of her son's attachment, and by her this was communicated to the Queen. An extract, sent at the same time, of a letter from the young Prince himself, produced such an impression upon the Queen and the Prince Consort that they felt bound to ascertain the state of their daughter's feelings. The result was such as to justify the encouragement of the young Prince's hopes. No engagement was made; but some months later Prince Louis was to return, and have an opportunity of pressing his suit in person. A few weeks later came the news that to the Princess Frederick William was born a daughter, and to the Queen and Prince a second grandchild. To the mother her father wrote on the 28th of July from Osborne: "The little girl must be a darling. Little girls are much prettier than boys. I advise her to model herself after her Aunt Beatrice. That excellent lady has not now a moment to spare. 'I have no time,' she says, when she is asked for anything; 'I must write letters to my niece.'"

On the 8th of August the Court arrived at Balmoral, and an interesting account is given, in the "Leaves from the Journal of our Life," of an expedition to Glen Fishie and Grantown. Attended by only Lady Churchill and General Grey, the Queen and Prince passed two days in the wildest scenery of the Highlands, traveling unrecognized as "Lord and Lady Churchill and party." Shortly after the return South, on the 22d of September, the Queen and the Prince Consort, with Princess Alice, left Gravesend in the Victoria and Albert, on their way to Coburg. Here they were welcomed by the Duke and Duchess of Saxe-Coburg Gotha, and had the additional delight of seeing again the Prince and Princess Frederick William of Prussia. But the festivities which were intended to enliven their visit were prevented by the death of the Dowager Duchess of Saxe-Coburg.

The Royal travelers left Coburg on the 12th of October, passing through Coblentz and Aix-la-Chapelle to Antwerp, where the yacht re-embarked her passengers and brought them to Gravesend on the 17th. During the stay at Coburg the Prince narrowly escaped a serious carriage accident. In thankfulness for his escape, the

Queen founded a permanent charity in the town of Coburg, from which a benevolent distribution should be
made annually on the 1st of October, the day of the
Prince's escape. This trust, called the Victoria-Stift
(Victoria foundation), still provides means for appren-
ticing or helping a number of young men and women
just entering life in the way of earning their own liveli-
hood. On the 9th of November Prince Alfred arrived
safely from his visit to the Cape, and on the 10th the
Prince of Wales returned home after his memorable visit
to Canada and the United States. On the 30th another
event of deep interest to the family took place, described
by the Queen in her Diary. "After dinner, while talking
to the gentlemen, I perceived Alice and Louis talking
before the fire-place more earnestly than usual, and,
when I passed to go to the other room, both came up to
me, and Alice in much agitation said he had proposed to
her, and he begged for my blessing. I could only
squeeze his hand and say 'Certainly,' and that we would
see him in our room later. Got through the evening,
working as well as we could; Alice came to our room
.   .   .   agitated but quiet.   .   .   .   Albert sent for
Louis to his room—went first to him, and then called
Alice and me in.   .   .   .   Louis has a warm, noble
heart." The welcome news of the satisfactory conclusion of the war with China contributed to the enjoyment
of the Christmas festivities at Windsor.

The condition of the country at the beginning of 1861,
when the Queen on the 5th of February opened Parliament in person, was tranquil and prosperous. Abroad
were difficulties, the most ominous being the rupture
between the northern and southern portions of the
United States; and the Italian question also caused the

Queen and Prince much anxiety. The 10th of February
was the twenty-first anniversary of the Queen's wedding,
of which the Queen wrote to her uncle as "a day which
has brought to us, and I may say to the world at large,
such incalculable blessings! Very few can say with me,
that this husband at the end of twenty-one years is not
only full of the friendship, kindness, and affection which
a truly happy marriage brings with it, but of the same
tender love as in the very first days of our marriage.
We missed dear mama and three of our children, but
had six dear ones round us." The Duchess of Kent,
who was so missed at this gathering, never again joined
the family circle. On the 15th of March the alarming
news was brought to Buckingham Palace that Her
Royal Highness had been seized with a shivering fit.
With all possible speed the Queen and Prince hastened
to Frogmore, to find the Duchess unconscious. She
passed away on the morning of the next day. The loss
of her mother was the deepest sorrow which the Queen
had ever felt. Writing to her uncle the same day, Her
Majesty says: "She is gone—that precious, dearly beloved, tender mother, whom I have never parted from
but for a few months—without whom I cannot imagine
life—has been taken from us! It is too dreadful! But
she is at peace!"

In this great sorrow the Queen was supported by a
husband's love. It was also no small consolation to feel
that the heart of the whole nation sympathized with her
in her loss. Addresses of condolence were voted in both
Houses of Parliament. "In the history of our reigning
house," said Mr. Disraeli, who seconded the Address in
the House of Commons, "none were ever placed as the
widowed Princess and her royal child. Never before

developed upon a delicate sex a more august or more awful responsibility. How these great duties were encountered—how fulfilled—may be read in the conscience of a grateful and a loyal people. Therefore the name of the Duchess of Kent will remain in our history from its interesting and benignant connection with an illustrious reign. For the great grief which has fallen upon the Queen there is only one source of human consolation—the recollection of unbroken devotedness to the being whom we have loved and whom we have lost. That tranquilizing and sustaining memory is the inheritance of our Sovereign. She who reigns over us has elected, amid all the splendor of Empire, to establish her life on the principle of domestic love. It is this, it is the remembrance and consciousness of this, which now sincerely saddens the public spirit, and permits a nation to bear its heartfelt sympathy to the foot of a bereaved throne, and to whisper solace to a royal heart."

The funeral of the Duchess took place on March 25th in St. George's Chapel, Windsor, where the remains were deposited till the completion of a mausoleum in the grounds of Frogmore. The death of the Duchess of Kent added much to the labors of the Prince Consort, upon whom unremitting work had begun seriously to tell. He was much occupied with the anxious state of affairs in Europe, and the preparations for the International Exhibition of 1862, which he was never to see, engaged much of his thoughts. When on the 5th of June he appeared, for the last time, at a public ceremonial, in order to open the Royal Horticultural Gardens at South Kensington, it was noticed how pale and worn he looked, and a much-needed move was made to Osborne, where the whole of July was passed.

On the 21st of August the Queen and Prince, with the Princesses Alice and Helena and Prince Alfred, crossed in the Royal yacht from Holyhead to Dublin. Landing next morning at Kingstown, they took up their residence in the Vice-regal Lodge in the Riding Park. On the 24th a grand review of about 10,000 troops in the Curragh Camp was held, but the spectacle was unfortunately spoiled by rain. Two days later they left Dublin, and spent some days in the enjoyment of the magnificent scenery at Killarney, where they stayed on a visit with Lord Kenmare at Kenmare House, and with Mr. Herbert at Muckross Abbey. On the 29th the journey was resumed by Dublin to Holyhead and on to Balmoral. In "Leaves from the Journal" details are given of the expeditions made by the Royal family through the Highlands in the same manner as those of the previous year. The description of that made on the 16th of October concludes with the words, "We returned at twenty minutes to seven o'clock, much pleased and interested with this delightful expedition. Alas! I fear our last great one!

(IT WAS OUR LAST ONE!—1867.)"

The Court returned to Windsor on the 24th of October. For a short time the Prince seemed to be in fair health, and was able to attend as usual to the many matters of interest that claimed his attention. The deaths of the young King of Portugal and his brother, however, within a few days of each other, gave him a severe shock. Still he continued, though feeling very unwell, and suffering much from sleeplessness, to take an active part in public affairs. On the 22d of November he went over to Sandhurst to inspect the buildings for the new Staff College and the Royal Military Academy, in which he had taken the keenest interest. The fatgue of this journey and the exposure to incessant rain had a most injurious effect. From this time he was in constant suffering from rheumatic pain, and to this were added the depression and weakness caused by continued want of sleep. On the 25th he paid, in cold and stormy weather, a visit to the Prince of Wales at Cambridge. On the 28th the alarming news arrived of the outrage by the Americans on the British flag, when the steamer Trent was boarded in mid-ocean by Captain Wilkes of the San Jacinto, and Messrs. Mason and Slidell, the envoys accredited by the Confederated States to England and to France, were removed by force from its protection. The news was received in England with such indignation and excitement, that to ordinary observers it appeared as if war was inevitable. It was then that the drafts of the despatches which it was proposed by the Cabinet to send to Lord Lyons at Washington were carefully read over by the Prince, and early in the morning of the 1st of December he was able, though suffering much from weakness, to draft the last memorandum that he ever wrote. The document led to the removal from the despatch of everything which could irritate a proud and sensitive nation, and afforded the United States an opportunity for receding from the position in which they had been placed by the overzealous action of their agent. The conciliatory tone of the amended despatch had its due effect; the news of the liberation of the prisoners reached London on the 9th of January, 1862, and was communicated to the Queen on the same day. Her Majesty, in the depth of her sorrow, replied: "Lord Palmerston cannot but look on this peaceful issue of the

American quarrel as greatly owing to her beloved Prince, who wrote the observations on the draft to Lord Lyons, in which Lord Palmerston so entirely concurred. It was the last thing he ever wrote." Lord Palmerston in his answer, on the 12th of January, wrote as follows:— "As Your Majesty observes, the alterations made in the despatch to Lord Lyons contributed essentially to the satisfactory settlement of the dispute. But these alterations were only one of innumerable instances of the tact and judgment, and the power of nice discrimination which excited Lord Palmerston's constant and unbounded admiration."

Meanwhile the Prince was slowly losing strength. He slept little, and could take no nourishment; but he rose and endeavored to exert himself. He had, on the 29th of November, witnessed the march past of the Eton College Volunteers, though conscious that his strength was overtaxed by the exertion. "Unhappily, I must be present," is the note in his Diary, and it is the last entry in it.

On the 7th of December typhoid fever was declared. All went well till the 12th, when the lungs became affected, and on the 14th the end came. By the bedside knelt the Queen, the Prince of Wales, the Princess Alice and Princess Helena. To quote the words of Sir Theodore Martin: "In the solemn hush of that mournful chamber there was such grief as has rarely hallowed any deathbed. A great light which had blessed the world, and which the mourners had but yesterday hoped might long bless it, was waning fast away. A husband, a father, a friend, a master, endeared by every quality by which man in such relations can win the love of his fellow-man, was passing into the Silent Land, and his loving glance, his wise counsels, his firm, manly thoughts

should be known among them no more. The Castle
clock chimed the third quarter after ten. Calm and
peaceful grew the beloved form; the features settled into
the beauty of a perfectly serene repose; two or three long,
but gentle, breaths were drawn; and that great soul had
fled, to seek a nobler scope for its aspirations in the world
within the veil, for which it had often yearned, where
there is rest for the weary, and where the spirits of the
just are made perfect."

CHAPTER EIGHT.

At midnight on the 14th of December, 1861, the tolling of the great bell of St. Paul's had announced to the citizens of London the mournful tidings of the Prince Consort's death, but large numbers of the people first learn, by the omission of the name from the Litany, what a blow had fallen on their Queen. On every side was heard the sympathetic outburst of grief for the Sovereign so early widowed.

The wreck of the Queen's domestic happiness, and the loss of that support which had divided the burthens and lightened the cares of sovereignty, were felt by all classes of her subjects as a private as well as public calamity. No such affliction had fallen upon the nation since the death of the Princess Charlotte, and the universal feeling of sorrow has never been surpassed in its depth and sincerity. In the general mourning for Princess Charlotte a note of sympathetic compassion was struck by the fate of a young and beautiful Princess suddenly removed at the most interesting crisis of a woman's life. The tribute which the nation paid to Prince Albert was different in character, though not less heartfelt. Gratitude for the great services which he had rendered to the country, for the example of moral purity he had displayed, and for the salutary influence he had exercised in his exalted station, admiration for his remarkable talents and accomplishments, respect for the wisdom with which he had kept himself clear from the conflicts of political parties, and appreciation of the self-effacing modesty with which he had so ably aided the Queen in all the affairs of State these were the sentiments that inspired the addresss of condolnce which were sent up from every part of the United Kingdom. To the addresses of the Houses of Parliament meeting in February, the Queen replied: "I return to you my most sincere thanks for your dutiful and affectionate address, especially for the manner in which you have assured me of your feelings on the irreparable loss sustained by mlself and the country, in the afflicting dispensation of Providence which bows me to the earth." But, prostrated as she was by the burthen of a sorrow which never could pass away, the Queen, strengthened by the cherished example of the loving counselor she had lost, resolutely overcame her physical exhaustion and the depression of inconsolable grief, and fulfilled those arduous duties, the performance of which she regarded as a sacred trust for her family and people. Speaking on this subject some years afterwards, a statesman of high rank remarked: "It is a circumstance worthy of observation, and which ought to be known to all the people of this country, that during all the years of the Queen's affliction, during which she has lived necessarily in comparative retirement, she has omitted no part of that public duty which concerns her as Sovereign of this country; and I am sure that when the Queen reapears on more public occasions. the people of this country will regard her only with increased affection, from the recollection that during all the time of her care and sorrow she has devoted herself, without one day's intermission, to those cares of government which belong to her position."

The funeral of the Prince Consort took place on Monday the 23rd of December, 1861, in St. George's Chapel. The remains were removed from the Castle and temporarily deposited in the entrance to the Royal Vault, where they were to remain until the completion and consecration of a mausoleum to be afterwards erected. The site for this building had been chosen by the Queen herself on the 18th, when with rPincess Alice she drove to the gardens at Frogmore for that purpose.

The Queen had before the funeral left Windsor to spend a sad and desolate Christmas at Osborne. Such consolation as was possible in a grief so overwhelming was afforded by the presence of the King of the Belgians and of the Princess of Hohenlohe, her half-sister. But Her Majesty had already learnt that the only anodyne to personal grief is sympathy with the sorrows of others. When the terrible disaster happened at Hartley Colliery, by which the whole male population of three hamlets had been swept away, Sir Charles Phipps writes by the Queen's command: "The appalling news has afflicted the Queen very much. Her Majesty commands me to say that her tenderest sympathy is with the poor widows and mothers, and that her own misery only makes her feel the more for them."

On the 6th of February, 1862, the Queen took leave of the Prince of Wales, who, in pursuance of the scheme for his education laid down by the Prince Consort, left England for the tour, which had been for some time arranged, to Egypt and the Holy Land. The most memorable incident of this tour was the visit paid by the Prince and his suite to the Mosque of Hebron, which covers the Cave of

Machpelah. Into this sacred building no European or Christian had been, up to this time, permitted to enter, and it was not without some difficulty, ½and even danger, that the visit was accomplished. It has been fully described by Dean Stanley, who accompanied the Prince on his journey. The party returned on the 14th of June, in time for the marriage of the Princess Alice with Prince Louis of Hesse.

At the time o fthe death of the rPince Consort, the Princess Alice had been the principal support of the broken-hearted Queen. Though herself filled with intense sorrow at the death of her beloved father, she became at once the means of communication between the outer world and her mother, whom she strove to shield from every possible trouble. The decision to leave Windsor for Osborne directly after the Prince's death, according to the earnest wish of the King of the Belgians, which it was so difficult for the Queen to make, was obtained by the rPincess's influence. For the Queen to part from one who had thus become necessary to her was a terrible struggle, but it had been the desire of the Prince Consort that the marriage should take place during the early part o fthe year, and it was, therefore, only postponed to the 1st of July, when it was solemnized at Osborne. Though the ceremony was simple and private, it may be doubted whether any royal marriage excited keener interest and profoundr sympathy in the mass of the people, who had so highly appreciated the strength of mind and self-sacrifice shown by the Princess Alice during the dreadful days of her father's illness and death, and who were aware that to her exertions it was to a great measure due that the Queen was able to bear with such fortitude her own irreparable loss.

The Queen passed the autumn in seclusion at Balmoral; here on the 21st of August was begun the cairn in memory of the Prince. In "More Leaves from the Journal" the Queen writes: "At eleven o'clock started * * * for Craig Lowrigan. . . . Here at the top is the foundation of the Cairn—forty feet wide—to be erected to my precious Albert, which will be seen all down the valley. I and my poor six orphans all placed stones on it; and our initials as well as those of the three absent ones are to be carved on stones all around it."

On the 1st of September the Queen, accompanied by several of her family, left England for Germany, paying on the way a brief visit to King Leopold . at Laeken There for the first time the Queen met the Princess Alexandra of Denmark, soon to become Princess of Wales. From Laeken the Queen went to Rheinhardtsbrunn in Thuringia, where she was joined by the Crown Prince and Princess of Prussia, by Princess Alice with her husband, and by Prince Alfred.

On the 18th of December, 1862, the remains of the Prince Consort were transferred from St. George's Chapel to the Mausoleum which had just been built for their reception by Her Majesty in the grounds of Frogmore, not far from the spot where the Duchess of Kent had been laid.

The Prince of Wales had met the Princess Alexandra at Heidelberg in the autumn of 1861, when a mutual attachment had been formed; but the death of the Prince Consort had postponed any announcement of an engagement. It was not till the 4th of November, 1862, that the Queen gave public consent to the marriage, and the Princess came for a brief visit to Osborne. In February,

1863, the Prince of Wales took the oath and his seat in the House of Lords, and in the House of Commons resolutions were passed for the establishment and maintenance of His Royal Highness's household on a proper scale. The alacrity shown by aPrliament in thus making a suitable provision expressed the universal feeling of satisfaction in the proposed union. The Prince had gained the personal regard of all those with whom he had been brought into contact, while the beauty and charm of the Princess won every heart. At the same time the alliance with Denmark, by the complete absence of State interests, and of those political aims to which the domestic happiness of princes has been too often sacrificed, strongly appealed to the sympathy of the nation.

The Princess landed at Gravesend on the 7th of March, and never to any person in the history of the kingdom has a warmer welcome been offered. Through the City, which was approached by London Bridge, there was one immense concourse of enthusiastic crowds. In Hyde Park were drawn up 17,000 volunteers, between whose ranks the procession passed to Paddington. The reception at Eton was as warm as that of London, and the illuminations at Windsor closed a memorable day. On the 10th the marriage was solemnized with great pomp in St. George's Chapel, the rPince and the other knights wearing their robes. The Queen herself took no part in the ceremony, but witnessed the whole from the windows of the Royal closet above the north side of the altar.

On the 9th of May the Queen, accompanied by the Princess Alice, paid a visit to the Military Hospital at Netley, the foundation stone of which she had, with the Prince Consort, laid nearly seven years before. Though

her features bore the traces of deep and abiding sorrow,
she bore with firmness the fatigue o fher long walk
through the hospital, and the trying scenes which she
witnessed. In August and September the Queen paid a
visit to Belgium and Germany, staying for some time
with King Leopold and passing on to the Rosenau, the
birthplace of the Prince Consort. On the journey home,
she spent a day with Princess Alice at Kranichstein, near
Darmstadt.

The first public appearance of the Queen since the
death of her hsuband was made on the 13th of October,
when Her Majesty unveiled the statue which had been
erected to the memory of the Prince Consort at Aberdeen. In her reply to the address of the Provost, the
Queen said: "I could not reconcile it to mlself to remain
at Balmoral while such a tribute was being paid to his
memory, without making an exertion to assure you personally of the deep and heartfelt sense I entertain of your
kindness and affection; and, at the same time, to proclaim
in public the unbounded reverence and admiration, the
devoted love that fills my heart for him whose loss must
throw a lasting gloom over all my future life."

On the 8th of January, 184, the Queen received at Osborne from the Prince of Wales the glad news of the
birth at Frogmore of a rPince, who, on the 10th of March
following the first anniversary of the wedding of his parents, was christened at Buckingham Palace, receiving
the names of Albert Victor Christian Edward. The ad-
vent of a male heir in direct succession to the Throne
was a source of much joy and consolation to the Queen
and to the Prince and Princess of Wales, as well as of
gratification to the whole nation.

On the 24th of May the anniversary of Her Majesty's birthday was kept this year with the old outward tokens of rejoicing, which had not been observed since the year 1861. On her way to Balmoral in the autumn, the Queen unveiled a statue which had been erected by her loyal subjects of Perth to the Prince Consort.

During the year 1865 the Queen remained in seclusion, attending to all affairs of State, but seldom appearing in public. On the 24th of March she visited the Consumpion Hospital at Brompton, the first stone of which had been laid by the Prince Consort in 1844. Her Majesty was much interested in the hospital, and spent some time in examining the wards and noticing the patients, of whom there were upwards of two hundred. On the 8th of August Her Majesty, accompanied by Prince Leopold and the Princesses Helena, Louise, and Beatrice, embarked at Woolwich for Germany, and, arriving at Coburg on the 11th, proceeded at once to Rosneau. On the 26th the Queen inaugurated the memorial statue which had been erected to her late husband in his native town. The solemn and elaborate ceremony reached its climax when the Queen, leaving her pavilion, walked with her family to the monument, and laid at the feet of the statue the flowers which she had brought for the purpose.

On her return homewards, the Queen saw for the last time her loved and respected uncle, King Leopold. He died at Laeken on the 9th of the following December, within a few days of completing his seventy-fifth year. Small and new as was his kingdom, he yet occupied a position which the most powerful monarch might envy. International disputes were referred to him for settle-

ment, the secrets of most royal houses were in his keeping, and private as well as public grievances were submitted to his arbitration; he was known everywhere by
the title of Juge de Paix de l'Europe. As son-in-law of
the King of the French and uncle of Queen Victoria, he
was able to mediate with great effect between the two
countries, both in 1840 on the Eastern question, and
later in the more irritating disputes about the Spanish
marriages. Throughout the whole of the Queen's life he
had been her trusted counsellor, confidant, and friend,
and his loss, following on that of her mother and her
husband, left her more completely alone.

A happier event this year was the birth on the 3rd of
June of the second son of the Prince and Princess of
Wales, now Duke of York. After the return of the Court
from Germany, the Queen spent the remainder of the
autumn at Balmoral, whence excursions were made to
Invermark and to Dunkeld to visit the wodowed Duchess
of Athole, who, whilst these pages are passing through
the press, has also been taken away.

On the 6th of February, 1866, the Queen, who since
the death of the Prince Consort had not entered the
walls of the Palace of Westminster, opened aPrliament
in person, to the great joy of both Houses and of all her
subjects. In the Speech from the Throne Her Majesty
declared her consent to the marriage of the Princess Helena with Prince Christian of Schleswig-Holstein-Sonder-
burg-Augustenburg, which marriage was solemnized on
the 5th of July in the private chapel of Windsor Castle.
On the 13th of March, after an interval of five years, the
Queen visited Aldershot and reviewed the troops there in
garrison. The visit was repeated on the 5th of April,

when new colours were presented by Her Majesty½ to the 89th Regiment, now the 2nd Battalion of the Princess Victoria's Royal Irish Fusiliers, the regiment to which the Queen, as Princess Victoria, had presented colours in 1833.

Affairs on the Continent at this time were a source of deep anxiety to the Queen, particularly because in the war between Austria and Prussia her tow sons-in-law, the husband of the Princess Royal and of Princess Alice, were engaged upon opposite sides. While the conflict was raging round her home Princess Alice gave birth to a daughter who, when the war came to an end, received the name of Irene.

On the 16th of October the Queen journeyed from Balmoral to Invercannie, twenty-two miles from Aberdeen, in order to open the new works just completed for the supply of water to the city. Of her reply to the address of the Provost, the Queen in "More Leaves from the Journal" writes: "Then I had to read my answer, which made me very nervous; but I got through it well, though it was the first time I had read anything since my darling husband was taken from me." In this answer the Queen said, "I have felt that, at a time when the attention of the country has been so anxiously directed to the state of the public health, it was right that I should make an exertion to testify my sense of the importance of a work so well calculated as this to promote the health and comfort of your ancient city."

At Wolverhampton, on the 30th of November, the Queen, accompanied by Prince and Princess Christian and Princess Louise, unveiled a statue to the Prince Consort.

On the 5th of February, 1867, the Queen was again able to open Parliament in person, the Speech from the Throne being, as on the former occasion, read by the Lord Chancellor. The aspect of affairs generally was gloomy: the cattle plague, the outbreak of the Fenian insurrection in Ireland, and the disturbances occasioned by the Reform agitation gave no promise of a prosperous year. The meetings held on the latter question, fortunately, passed over without riot, though considerable apprehension was felt.

The first stone of the Albert Hall at Kensington, adjoining the gardens of the Horticultural Society, was laid by the Queen on the 20th of May. The building was finished in 1871, when the Queen performed the opening ceremony.

Among the events of the year 1867 none is more memorable than the visit which the Sultan Abdul Azziz paid to England in July. It was the first time that any "Commander of the Faithful" had set foot on British ground. His Majesty was lodged at Buckingham Palace, and on the day following his arrival paid a visit to the Queen at Windsor before her departure for Osborne. On the 17th of July what had been intended to be the most interesting of all the spectacles offered to the Sultan—a naval review at Spithead—was marred by stormy weather. Forty-nine vessels mounting 1,099 guns were anchored in two columns, through which the Royal yachts passed with the Imperial and Royal visitors. On the deck of the Victoria and Albert the Queen invested the Sultan with the Order of the Garter. Having again visited the Royal Victoria Hospital at Netley, in which her interest was unabated, the Queen on the 20th of August left Osborne for Balmoral, stopping at the

Border to pay a visit to the Duke and Duchess of Roxburgh at Floors Castle. During the stay here Melrose Abbey and Abbotsford were visited, where the Queen wrote her name in Sir Walter Scott's journal, "which," as she says in "More Leaves from the Journal," "I felt it to be a presumption in me to do." During the stay at Balmoral an excursion was made to Glenfiddich, a graphic description of which is given in the same "Journal." On the 15th of October, the day of the Queen's engagement, the statue erected in memory of the Prince was unveiled at Balmoral.

In March of the following year the Queen was much alarmed by the news from New South Wales that an attempt to assassinate the Duke of Edinburgh had been made at Port Jackson. Succeeding telegrams fortunately confirmed the news that the Duke's condition was favorable and that no danger was anticipated. This dastardly attack caused universal horror and indignation throughout Australia. Opening the new buildings of St. Thomas's Hospital on the banks of the Thames opposite to the Houses of Parliament, on the 13th of May, Her Majesty feelingly acknowledged the sympathy shown to her by the nation in her distress. In June, 1868, 27,000 Volunteers were reviewed in the Great Park at Windsor; and on the 5th of August Her Majesty, travelling as the Countess of Kent, left Osborne for Cherbourg, passing through Paris to Lucerne, where she remained with Prince Leopold and the Princesses Louise and Beatrice for a month. Returning through Paris, the happy memories of earlier days were recalled by a short visit to St. Cloud. Windsor was reached on the 11th of September, and three days afterwards the Court left for Balmoral. During this visit the Glassalt Shiel, so well known as a favorite resort of the Queen, was occupied for the first time.

It was about this time widely rumoured that the Queen intended to take her former place in social life. In order to contradict this unfounded report a special notice was published in The Times: "An erroneous impression seems generally to prevail, and has lately found frequent expression in the newspapers, that the Queen is about to resume the place in society which she occupied before her great affliction; that is, that she is about to hold levees and drawing-rooms in person, and to appear as before at Court balls, concerts, etc. This idea cannot be too explicitly contradicted.

"The Queen appreciates the desire of her subjects to see her, and whatever she can do to gratify them in this loyal and affectionate wish she will do. Whenever any real object is to be obtained by her appearing on public occasions, any national interest to be promoted, or anything to be encouraged which is for the good of the people, Her Majesty will not shrink, as she has not shrunk, from any personal sacrifice or exertion, however painful.

"But there are other and higher duties than those of mere representation which are now thrown upon the Queen alone and unassisted—duties which she cannot neglect without injury to the public service—which weigh unceasingly upon her, overwhelming her with work and anxiety. The Queen has laboured conscientiously to discharge these duties till her health and strength, already shaken by the bitter and abiding desolation which has taken the place of her former happiness, have been impaired.

"To call upon her to undergo, in addition, the fa-

tigue of those mere State ceremonies, which can be
equally well performed by other members of her family,
is to ask her to run the risk of entirely disabling herself
for the discharge of those other duties, which cannot be
neglected without serious injury to the public interests.
The Queen will, however, do what she can—in the manner least trying to her health, strength and spirits—to
meet the loyal wishes of her subjects; to afford that support and countenance to society, and to give that encouragement to trade, which is desired of her. More the
Queen cannot do; and more the kindness and good feeling of her people will surely not exact of her."

Her Majesty has more than redeemed this promise,
though, as years have passed, the mass of business which
she alone can transact has almost daily increased in volume. This necessary work could only be mastered by
the strictest economy of time. Wherever the Queen is
residing, whether at home or abroad, the same method
and regularity are maintained. Nor has she failed to
answer those special demands which have been made by
the ceremonies attached to the commencement or completion of works of public importance. Holborn Via-
duct, the buildings of the London University, the new
wing of the London Hospital, the new Law Courts, the
People's Palace at Mile End, the Imperial Institute, were
opened by Her Majesty in person. In her presence Ep-
ping Forest was dedicated to the use of the public for
all time. By her hand was laid the foundation stone of
the new Medical Hall of the Royal College of Physicians
and Surgeons on the Thames Embankment. By opening the Colonial and Indian Exhibition at South Kensington the Queen showed how great was her interest
in the welfare of these branches of her Empire, and her
desire that they should be better known to her subjects

at home. In the provinces the Queen has also endeavoured to promote the same spirit of public activity. At Birmingham she laid the foundation stone of the new Law Courts, and at Derby of the Infirmary; at Manchester she opened the Ship Canal; at Glasgow and at Sheffield the new municipal buildings; at Liverpool the International Exhibition; at Southampton the deep docks.

These instances illustrate the many-sided sympathies of the Queen in national life as a whole. Her Majesty has also, at all times, proved her warm appreciation of the loyalty of her subjects who have entered into her own service. Her interest in the navy has been great and exhibited wherever a suitable opportunity has presented itself. Thus, in 1878, and again in 1887 on the occasion of the Jubilee, when 134 ships of various descriptions were collected at Spithead, she reviewed the fleet, and in 1891 she visited Portsmouth to christen and launch the Royal Sovereign, the largest ironclad afloat, and the Royal Arthur, a new and powerful cruiser. For reviews of troops opportunities have more frequently occurred. Aldershot and its garrison has been many times honoured by the presence of the Queen; at Windsor also the Queen has reviewed her regular troops, taking advantage of the visit of the Shah of Persia to assemble there some 10,000 men, and in July, 1881, Her Majesty reviewed the English volunteers, then celebrating their majority, when upwards of 50,000 marched past. This review was followed by another at Edinburgh in the following month, when 40,000 volunteers of the North paraded before the Queen. The 79th Cameron Highlanders and the 2d Battalion of the Berkshire Regiment received new colours from the Queen's hands in the Isle of Wight, and at Windsor the 4th Regiment was similarly honoured.

In 1876 the Queen was able, for the second time since her widowhood, to open Parliament in person on the 8th of February. In the Speech from the Throne occurred the following passage: "At the time that the direct government of my Indian Empire was transferred to the Crown, no formal addition was made to the style and title of the Sovereign. I have deemed the present a fitting opportunity for supplying this omission, and a Bill upon the subject will be presented to you." This Bill was introduced in the House of Commons by Mr. Disraeli on the 17th of February. The title selected by the Queen was "Empress of India." The Bill was resisted with some show of vigour by the Opposition, but was eventually passed, and received the Royal assent. The proclamation of the new title was made on the 1st of May by the Sheriffs of London and Middlesex, and also at Edinburgh. The formal proclamation of the Empire in India took place on New Year's Day, 1877, at Calcutta, Bombay, Madras and Delhi. At the last-named place the Viceroy, Lord Lytton, presided at a magnificent Durbar, when sixty-three ruling chiefs were assembled.

At the opening of Parliament by Her Majesty in person on the 8th of February, the Queen's Speech contained this paragraph: "My assumption of the Imperial title at Delhi was welcomed by the chiefs and people of India with professions of affection and loyalty most grateful to my feelings." In commemoration of the event, a large gold medal was struck, copies of which were presented to the native chiefs and the principal officials of the new Empire. An illustration of this medal is on page 159. At the same time, the Queen founded the Most Eminent Order of the Indian Empire, in addition to the Most Exalted Order of the Star of India, which had been instituted by Her Majesty in 1865 after the termination of the Indian Mutiny, and to the Order of the Crown of India for ladies, and especially for ladies connected with the Indian Empire. The insignia of the two first of these orders are also represented in the illustration on page 159.

Among other Orders instituted or enlarged during the Queen's reign, mention should be made of the Order of "Victoria and Albert," originally worn as a badge by Royal Ladies and Princesses of the Queen's family, but created an Order in 1862. Another Order is the Most Distinguished Order of St. Michael and St. George. Originally instituted in 1818 in connection with the Ionian Islands, it was enlarged in 1868, and again in 1877, for subjects of the Crown who had held high and confidential offices within Her Majesty's Colonial possessions, or for service in relation to the Foreign affairs of the Empire. In 1886 the Queen created a new naval and military order for the reward of individual instances of meritorious or distinguished service in the field or before the enemy; this is called "the Distinguished Service Order." Mention has been made earlier of the institution in 1856 of the Victoria Cross for rewarding individual acts of heroism in war. Ten years afterward the Queen instituted the Albert Medal for the purpose of rewarding by royal favour the many daring and heroic actions performed by mariners and others in saving life at sea. By another warrant a year later, in 1877, this decoration was extended to cases of gallantry in preventing loss of life from accidents in mines, at fires, and other perils on shore. These are illustrated on page 73. On the 21st of April, 1896, the Queen instituted the Royal Victorean Order (illustrated on page 195), to be conferred as a mark of high distinction upon those who have rendered personal service to Her Majesty.

In the long course of years, uniformly occupied with the laborious discharge of the complicated business of the State, and marked by special efforts to encourage national movements, or to promote the efficiency of the public services, the Queen has witnessed many changes, some happy, some painful, in the expanding circle of her domestic life.

In the autumn of the year 1870 the Queen in Council gave her consent to the marriage of Princess Louise with the Marquis of Lorne, eldest son of the Duke of Argyll. The engagement had taken place at Balmoral in October, and the marriage ceremony was solemnized, on the 21st of March, 1871, in St. George's Chapel, Windsor, the Queen herself giving away the bride.

The next marriage of one of Her Majesty's children was that of the Duke of Edinburgh, who, on the 23d of January, 1874, was united at St. Petersburg to the Grand Duchess Marie Alexandrovna, only daughter of the Emperor Alexander II. This was the first alliance ever formed between the royal houses of England and Russia, and the Princess was received, on her arrival in England, with the warmest welcome. It was the first time also that, since the Act of Settlement, a British Prince had taken a wife not belonging to the Protestant communion; but in that Act the Greek Church was not mentioned, so no objection was made to the daughter of the Emperor of Russia retaining her allegiance to her own faith when she became Duchess of Edinburgh.

Five years later, the Queen saw the marriage of another son. On the 13th of March, 1879, the Duke of Connaught was married, at St. George's Chapel, Windsor, to the Princess Louise Margaret of Prussia, daughter of Prince Frederick Charles of Prussia, well known as "the Red Prince." In this same year, on the 12th of May, the Queen's first great-grandchild, a daughter of the Princess Charlotte of Saxe-Meiningen, daughter of the Princess Royal, was born.

On the 27th of April, 1882, Prince Leopold, Duke of Albany, the youngest, and only unmarried, son of the Queen, was married at St. George's Chapel to the Princess Helen of Waldeck-Pyrmont. Only a few days before the ceremony, a man named Maclean had been tried and convicted for the cowardly outrage of firing at Her Majesty, as she with Princess Beatrice was leaving Windsor Station.

One only of the Queen's children was now unmarried, the youngest Princess. Since her father's death, Princess Beatrice, who was then four years old, had been the daily companion of her mother, and the knowledge of the dutiful manner in which she had watched by Her Majesty, and done her utmost to cheer and lighten the solitude of her life, had given her a strong hold on the affection of the nation. It was therefore with no little interest that, in 1885, at the beginning of the year, the announcement was received that the Queen had approved of her marriage with Prince Henry of Battenberg. The Prince was no stranger to the family, as his eldest brother, Prince Louis, had already married the Princess Victoria of Hesse, eldest daughter of the Grand Duke of

Hesse and Princess Alice, and was a distinguished officer in Her Majesty's Navy. The marriage was performed at Whippingham Church, on the 23d of July, 1885; but, unlike the marriages of the Queen's other children, it entailed no separation from her daughter, who with her husband continued to live with Her Majesty wherever she resided.

Although in these additions to her family the Queen had found much happiness and consolation, yet sorrow and suffering have rarely been long absent, and successive losses have left gaps in the circle never to be filled, and memories never to be forgotten. The Queen passed through a time of terrible trial and anxious suspense when the Prince of Wales, on the 23rd of November, 1871, was attacked by typhoid fever. So grave were the symptoms that the Queen on the 29th, having just returned from Balmoral, determined to go to Sandringham, where the Prince was lying. The Princess Louis of Hesse was there also on a visit to her brother, and it was fresh in the memories of a sympathizing nation how assiduous her attentions had been, just ten years before, when her lamented father lay dying from a fever of the same nature. The intensity of public feeling was allayed for a time by reports of the normal course of the disease; but it was deepened on the 8th of December, when a serious relapse occurred, and the Queen, who had returned to Windsor on the 1st, hurried back to Sandringham to watch over her son. On the 10th, by Her Majesty's desire, forms of prayer for the recovery of the Heir to the Throne were issued by the Archbishop of Canterbury, and religious communities of all kinds throughout the Empire joined in the universal intercession. It was not till December the 14th, the anniversary of the Prince Consort's death, that the illness took a favorable turn, and from that day the Prince slowly but surely recovered. The loyalty and sympathy shown to the Queen by her subjects in this time of trial were acknowledged in the following letter:—

"Windsor Castle, December 26th, 1871.

"The Queen is very anxious to express her deep sense of the touching sympathy of the whole nation on the occasion of the alarming illness of her dear son the Prince of Wales. The universal feeling shown by her people during those painful, terrible days, and the sympathy evinced by them with herself and her beloved daughter the Princess of Wales, as well as the general joy in the improvement of the Prince of Wales's state, have made a deep and lasting impression upon her heart which can never be effaced. It was, indeed, nothing new to her, for the Queen had met with the same sympathy when, just ten years ago, a similar illness removed from her side the best, wisest, and kindest of husbands.

"The Queen wishes to express, at the same time, on behalf of the Princess of Wales, her feelings of heartfelt gratitude, for she has been as deeply touched as the Queen by the great and universal manifestations of loyalty and sympathy.

"The Queen cannot conclude without expressing her hope that her faithful subjects will continue their prayers to God for the complete recovery of her dear son to health and strength."

This letter addressed to her subjects aroused among the people a deep feeling. Each one read it as a personal acknowledgment, and the warmth of affection to their

Sovereign and family was manifested by the spontaneity and sincerity of the national thanksgiving for the restoration to health of the Prince of Wales, which was held on the 27th of February, 1872. This service had at first been arranged more as a private act of devotion on the part of the Queen and her household; but it assumed, day by day, the proportions of a national festival, until it culminated in the grandest outburst of unanimous popular emotion which had been witnessed since the times of the Tudors.

Two days after the ceremony at St. Paul's, the following letter was published in the London Gazette:—

"Buckingham Palace, February 29th, 1872.

"The Queen is anxious, as on a previous occasion, to express publicly her own personal very deep sense of the reception she and her dear children met with on Tuesday, February 27th, from millions of her subjects on her way to and from St. Paul's.

"Words are too weak for the Queen to say how very deeply touched and gratified she has been, by the immense enthusiasm and affection exhibited towards her dear son and herself, from the highest down to the lowest, on the long progress through the capital, and she would earnestly wish to convey her warmest, and most heartfelt thanks, to the whole nation for this great demonstration of loyalty.

"The Queen, as well as her son and her dear daughter-in-law, felt that the whole nation joined them in thanking God for sparing the beloved Prince of Wales's life.

"The remembrance of this day, and of the remarkable order maintained throughout, will for ever be affectionately remembered by the Queen and her family."

Another period of deep suspense and anxiety, fortunately coming, like the illness of the Prince of Waltes, to a joyful termination, was the Egyptian war of 1882, which brought home to Her Majesty the anxiety and suspense inseparable from those who have near and dear relatives in the field. The Queen has always watched the movements of her brave sailors and soldiers with a tender and anxious care; but it was not till September, 1882, that one of her own sons was under fire in a distant land. An English army had been despatched to Egypt to assist the Khedive in the subjugation of his rebellious army under Arabi Pasha. The troops were commanded by Sir Garnet, now Lord, Wolseley, and under him the Duke of Connaught was in command of the brigade of Guards. The Egyptian army, in a strongly entrenched position at Tel-el-Kebir, awaited the final attack of the British troops, which was delivered on the 12th of September. In "More Leaves from the Journal" the Queen writes:—

"Monday, September 11, 1882.

"Received a telegram in cypher from Sir John McNeill (who was on the Duke's personal staff), marked very secret, saying that it was 'determined to attack the enemy with a very large force on Wednesday.' How anxious this made us, God only knows; and yet this long delay had already intensified our suspense. No one to know, though all expected something at the time."

"Tuesday, September 12.

". . . I prayed earnestly for my darling child, and longed for the morrow to arrive. Read Korner's beautiful Gebet von der Schlacht, 'Vater, ich rufe Dich' (Prayer before the battle, 'Father, I call on Thee'). My beloved husband used to sing it often. My thoughts were entirely fixed on Egypt and the coming battle. My nerves were strained to such a pitch by the intensity of my anxiety and suspense that they seemed to feel as though they were all alive."

"Wednesday, September 13th.

". . . Took my short walk and breakfasted in the cottage. Had a telegram that the army marched out last night. What an anxious moment! . . . Another telegram, also from Reuter, saying that fighting was going on, and that the enemy had been routed with heavy losses at Tel-el-Kebir. Much agitated.

"On coming in got a telegram from Sir John McNeill, saying, 'A great victory; Duke safe and well.' Sent all to Louischen (the Duchess of Connaught). The excitement was very great. Felt unbounded joy and gratitude for God's great goodness and mercy. . . . A little later, just before two, came the following most welcome and gratifying telegram from Sir Garnet Wolseley:

" 'Ismalia, September 13th, 1882.

" 'Attacked Arabi's position at five this morning. His strongly entrenched position was most bravely and gallantly stormed by the Guards and line, while cavalry and horse artillery worked round their left flank. At seven o'clock I was in complete possession of his whole camp. . . . Enemy completely routed, and his losses have been very heavy; also regret to say we have suffered severely. Duke of Connaught is well and behaved admirably, heading his brigade to the attack.'

"Brown brought the telegrams, and followed me to Beatrice's room, where Louischen was, and I showed it to her. I was myself quite upset, and embraced her warmly, saying what joy and pride and cause of thankfulness it was to know our darling was safe, and so much praised! I feel quite beside myself for joy and gratitude, though grieved to think of our losses, which, however, have not proved to be so serious as first reported. We were both much overcome. . . . A telegram from Sir Garnet Wolseley to Mr. Childers, with fuller accounts, arrived. The loss, thank God! is not so heavy as we feared at first. A bonfire was to be lit by my desire at the top of Craig Gowan at nine, just where there had been one in 1856, after the fall of Sebastopol, when dearest Albert went up to it at night with Bertie and Affie. That was on September 13th, very nearly the same time, twenty-six years ago." That very day, a few hours afterwards, the Duke of Albany arrived with his bride.

On the 23d of September, 1872, the Queen received the distressing news of the death, at Baden-Baden, of her sister, the Dowager Princess of Hohenlohe-Langenburg. The declining health of the Princess had been for some time a source of anxiety, but so rapid a termination of the illness was unexpected, and was a painful shock to Her Majesty, who lost a most affectionate sister to whom she had always been warmly attached.

Six years later, came a yet deeper sorrow, when the first of the Queen's own children was to follow the husband and father into the silent land—Princess Alice, Grand Duchess of Hesse, who had been taken ill on the 7th of December, 1878, with diphtheria, caught in attendance upon her husband and upon her children, all of whom, except Princess Elizabeth, now the Grand Duchess Elizabeth of Russia, had suffered, and one of whom had died from the illness. Her own sufferings

were borne with wonderful patience, and at first it was
believed that her life might be spared; but it was not to
be, and on the fatal 14th of December she died, murmur-
ing to herself, "From Friday to Saturday, four weeks—
May—dear Papa—!" It was exactly four weeks to the
day since her child, Princess Marie, known to her family
by the pet name of May, had died, and seventeen years
since the death of the Prince Consort. In her grief the
Queen had the warm sympathy of the whole nation,
which well remembered the devotion of the Princess to
her father in the illness from which he died, and to her
brother during that from which he mercifully recovered.
In the land of her adoption her loss was equally deplored,
for there she had won the love of the people by her constant care for their interests, more especially during the
trying times of the Franco-German War, when the sick
and wounded learned to bless her name as their com-
forter and friend. Her remains were laid to rest in the
mausoleum at Rosenhohe, where a tomb, bearing a recumbent effigy by Boehm, representing the Princess
holding in her arms the Princess Marie, is now placed.
This effigy was copied from that which adorns the mausoleum of the Prince Consort at Frogmore. A memorial
of another kind is to be found in the "Biographical
Sketch and Letters of the Princess," so ably edited by
her sister, Princess Helena, Princess Christian of Schles-
wig-Holstein, in which it can be seen that the love of
husband and children, only deepened the affection which
she had for her loved and widowed mother.

The following letter from the Queen appeared in the
London Gazette:—

"Osborne, December 26th, 1878.
"The Queen is anxious to take the earliest oppor-

tunity of expressing publicly her heartfelt thanks for the universal and most touching sympathy shown to her by all classes of her loyal and faithful subjects on the present occasion, when it has pleased God to call from this world her dearly-beloved daughter, the Princess Alice, Grand Duchess of Hesse. Overwhelmed with grief at the loss of a dear child, who was a bright example of loving tenderness, courageous devotion, and self-sacrifice to duty, it is most soothing to the Queen's feelings to see how entirely her grief is shared by her people. The Queen's deeply afflicted son-in-law, the Grand Duke of Hesse, is also anxious to make known his sincere gratitude for the kind feelings expressed towards himself and his dear children in their terrible bereavement, and his gratification at the appreciation shown by the people of England of the noble and endearing qualities of her whom all now mourn. Seventeen years ago, at this very time, when a similar bereavement crushed the Queen's happiness, and this beloved and lamented daughter was her great comfort and support, the nation evinced the same touching sympathy, as well as when, in December, 1871, the Prince of Wales was at the point of death. Such an exhibition of true and tender feeling will ever remain engraven on the Queen's heart, and is more to be valued at this moment of great distress in the country, which no one more deeply deplores than the Queen herself."

At the funeral of the Princess Alice, two of her brothers were present—the eldest, whose recovery she had herself witnessed, and the youngest, who was fated to follow her. Prince Leopold had, from his early years, been always of delicate constitution—as the Princess Alice had said, he had been three times given back to his family from the brink of the grave. Living a retired and studious life, he gave promise of succeeding to his father's position as head of all progressive movements in literature and art. Trained while young at home, in 1872 he went, at his own particular wish, to Oxford, and matriculated at Christ Church. Here he mixed freely with those of his own age, but he equally cultivated the society of those older in years who were distinguished in literature and science. He was sworn of the Privy Council in 1874, and later received a commission in the army and the command of the Seaforth Highlanders. In the debates of the House of Lords, which he entered as Duke of Albany in 1881, he took little part, though his interest in the politics of the day was keen and intelligent, but he made a great reputation as a public speaker, particularly in London, and at Manchester, where he pleaded the cause of music and education. His health, as he grew older, so much improved, that it was hoped he might be able to throw off his constitutional weakness; but after two years of married happiness he died suddenly at Cannes, on the 28th of March, 1884, leaving his widow with one daughter. A son was born to him, after his death, on the 19th of July. His remains were brought over to England, and he now lies in the Albert Chapel at Windsor, within the sound of the organ he loved so well when alive. A most touching tribute to his memory is the poem call "The Untravelled Traveller," by Dean Stanley, originally written in 1875, and reprinted at the time of his death.

On the eve of her departure for the Continent to be present at the marriage of her grand-daughter, Princess Victoria of Hesse, with Prince Louis of Battenberg, the Queen, through the Home Secretary, addressed the following letter to her people:—

"Windsor Castle, April 14th, 1884.

"I have on several previous occasions given personal expression to my deep sense of the loving sympathy and loyalty of my subjects in all parts of my Empire. I wish, therefore, in my present grievous bereavement, to thank them most warmly for the very gratifying manner in which they have shown not only their sympathy with me and my dear so-deeply-afflicted daughter-in-law, and my other children, but also their high appreciation of my beloved son's great qualities of head and heart, and of the loss he is to the country and to me. The affectionate sympathy of my loyal people, which has never failed me in weal or woe, is very soothing to my heart.

"Though much shaken and sorely afflicted by the many sorrows and trials which have fallen upon me during these past years, I will not lose courage, and, with the help of Him who has never forsaken me, will strive to labor on for the sake of my children, and for the good of the country I love so well, as long as I can.

"My dear daughter-in-law, the Duchess of Albany, who bears her terrible misfortune with the most admirable, touching, and unmurmuring resignation to the will of God, is also deeply gratified by the universal sympathy and kind feeling evinced towards her.

"I would wish, in conclusion, to express my gratitude to all other countries for their sympathy—above all, to the neighboring one where my beloved son breathed his last, and for the great respect and kindness shown on that mournful occasion.

"VICTORIA R. AND I."

A recumbent effigy of Sir Edgar Boehm, R. A., of the lamented Prince, in his uniform as Colonel of the Seaforth Highlanders, has been placed on his tomb.

It has been one consequence of the early age at which the Queen came to the throne that the friends and associates of her youth have passed away, and latterly in greater numbers. The catalogue of these is long and recalls many sad memories. Among the ladies of the Court who have been closely connected with Her Majesty, may be mentioned the Duchess of Sutherland, Lady Jocelyn, Lady Caroline Barrington, Lady Augusta Stanley, Lady Gainsborough, Lady Ely, the Duchess of Roxburghe, and the Duchess of Athole; among other members of the Royal household who have served their Royal Mistress with single-minded devotion, the names of General the Hon. Charles Grey, the Hon. Sir Charles Phipps, Sir Thomas Biddulph, Sir John Cowell, and Sir Henry Ponsonby rise to the memory immediately.

The thoughtful kindness which the Queen has always shown to her servants, and the implicit confidence which she has reposed in their loyalty, have won from those in her employment that devoted personal service which has so long distinguished her domestic establish-- ment. Among those who, by their tried fidelity, have thus earned and enjoyed her trust, Mrs. Macdonald and John Brown may be taken as types, both of whom passed upwards of thirty years in close and daily attendance upon Her Majesty.

The 20th of June, 1887, was the fiftieth anniversary of the Queen's accession. Three times only in the history of the country had the reign of an English Sovereign attained this number of years, and Her Majesty's Jubilee was celebrated throughout the Empire with universal rejoicing. No preceding half-century had ever witnessed such striking progress in the prosperity and power of a nation, and it was deemed fitting that this anniversary should be celebrated with all the loyalty and enthusiasm which a united people could evince towards a Sovereign who, through weal and woe, had presided with such wisdom and prudence over the councils of the State, had set so beneficent an example of domestic virtue, and had so closely identified herself with the joys and sorrows of all her subjects.

On the 21st of June the Queen, accompanied by her children and grandchildren, and attended by a number of foreign Sovereigns or their representatives, went in State from Buckingham Palace to Westminster Abbey, where a special service was held. Her Majesty's carriage, escorted by a brilliant body of officers of Indian Cavalry, was preceded by a cortege of Princes all nearly related to the Queen, conspicuous among whom towered the Crown Prince of Germany in the white uniform of the Prussian Gardes du Corps. A picture of this cavalcade, as it passed to Westminster through Trafalgar Square, has been painted for the Queen by Mr. Charlton, and is here reproduced.

Since the Coronation the Abbey had never seen so impressive a spectacle. The Queen sate in the chair of Edward the Confessor, in which, fifty years before, she had been crowned; the Abbey was filled with a brilliant throng, and the service of thanksgiving was striking and magnificent. The "Te Deum" was sung by three hundred voices to the music of the Prince Consort, and a special Jubilee anthem, composed by Dr. (now Sir John Frederick) Bridge, was also performed. At the conclusion of the service, which had been conducted by the Archbishop of Canterbury, Dr. Benson, the Queen kissed each of her children and retired, passing to Buckingham Palace amid the renewed greetings of her subjects.

To the Home Secretary after this event the Queen addressed the following letter:

"Windsor Castle, June 24.

"I am anxious to express to my people my warm thanks for the kind, and more than kind, reception I met with on going to, and returning from, Westminster Abbey, with all my children and grandchildren.

"The enthusiastic reception I met with then, as well as on these eventful days in London as well as in Windsor, on the occasion of my Jubilee, has touched me most deeply. It has shown that the labors and anxiety of fifty long years, twenty-two of which I spent in unclouded happiness shared and cheered by my beloved husband, while an equal number were full of sorrows and trials, borne without his sheltering arm and wise help, have been appreciated by my people.

"This feeling, and the sense of duty towards my dear country and subjects, who are so inseparably bound up with my life, will encourage me in my task, often a very difficult and arduous one, during the remainder of my life.

"The wonderful order preserved on this occasion, and the good behavior of the enormous multitudes assembled, merits my highest admiration.

"That God may protect and abundantly bless my country is my fervent prayer.

"VICTORIA, R. AND I."

On the 2d of July, 1887, the Queen, at Buckingham Palace, saw a march-past of over 23,000 Volunteers, and two days later Her Majesty laid the foundation stone of the Imperial Institute. In her reply to the address from the organizing committee, read by the Prince of Wales, the Queen said: "I concur with you in thinking that the counsel and exertions of my beloved husband initiated a movement which gave increased vigor to commercial activity, and produced marked and lasting improvements in industrial efforts. One indirect result of that movement has been to bring more before the minds of men the vast and varied resources of the Empire over which Providence has willed that I should reign during fifty prosperous years. I believe and hope that the Imperial Institute will play a useful part in combining those resources for the common advantage of all my subjects, and conducing toward the welding of the Colonies, India, and the Mother Country into one harmonious and united community."

On the 9th of July the Queen reviewed her troops, 58,000 men with 102 guns, at Aldershot. Before the march-past the Queen received from the Duke of Cambridge, Commander-in-Chief, the congratulations of the army on her Jubilee, to which Her Majesty returned a gracious reply.

On the 23d of the same month, a great naval review at Spithead concluded the Jubilee celebrations. The fleet consisted of one hundred and thirty-five vessels, mounting about five hundred guns, with a complement of officers and men of twenty thousand. After passing through the line, Her Majesty summoned the commanders of the ships on board the royal yacht, and expressed to each the satisfaction the display had given

her, and her appreciation of the hearty reception accorded to her by the crews.

On the 15th of the same month, the Queen, before
leaving Windsor, laid at Smith's Lawn, in the Great
Park, the foundation stone of the equestrian statue of
the Prince Consort presented by the women and girls
of the United Kingdom; the surplus of this Jubilee offering was, by Her Majesty's decision, devoted to the
benefit of nurses and nursing establishments—a much-
needed movement of practical utility, which had for
some time engaged Her Majesty's serious attention,
and had been fostered by her daughter Princess Christian, who has spared neither time nor trouble in promoting its success.

Among those nearest and dearest to the Queen,
who took part in the Jubilee of 1887, four have since
passed away—the Emperor Frederic, the Grand Duke
of Hesse, the Duke of Clarence, and Prince Henry of
Battenberg.

The Crown Prince of Germany, who had for some
time suffered from an affection of the larynx, passed
the winter of 1887-88 at San Remo, and only left for
Berlin on the 10th of March, 1888, when he received
the news of his accession to the throne of Prussia and
of the German Empire, by the death of his father the
day before. The malady from which he suffered, notwithstanding the strenuous efforts of his medical attendants, continued to increase in an alarming manner,
though his own vitality and courage at times gave
hope of amendment. He battled bravely against fate,
but on the 15th of June the end came, and after a short
reign of ninety-nine days, the Emperor Frederic, whose

noble character was fitly shrined in a commanding figure and a stately presence, was lost to his sorrowing
family and to his country, and the Queen's eldest daughter was left a widow. The Queen had paid a visit to
her son-in-law at Charlottenburg on the 24th of April,
where she had the melancholy satisfaction of seeing him
during one of the temporary rallies.

Another Prince, who had taken part in the procession of 1887, was the Grand Duke of Hesse. Though
less known in England than the Crown Prince of Prussia, the Grand Duke had been closely associated with
the Queen in many happy hours of her life, and his
death, which severed another link with the golden past,
was deeply felt by Her Majesty, who was warmly attached to the husband of Princess Alice.

A loss which appealed more directly to the British
people was that of the Duke of Clarence and Avondale,
the eldest son of the Prince and Princess of Wales, and
ultimate heir to the throne. Attacked by the prevailing epidemic of influenza in January, 1892, he was unable to struggle against the complication of pneumonia,
which set in at an early stage of his illness. On January
14th he died—a few days after his birthday and within a
few weeks of his marriage. Youth, brilliant position,
and his approaching marriage, lent peculiar pathos to
the death of the Duke, whose loss was deeply felt by his
parents and his grandmother. He was buried in the
Albert Chapel at Windsor on January 20, 1892. On the
same day the Queen wrote from Osborne to the Home
Secretary as follows:

"I must once again give expression to my deep
sense of the loyalty and affectionate sympathy evinced

by my subjects in every part of my Empire on an occasion more sad and tragical than any but one which has befallen me and mine, as well as the nation. The overwhelming misfortune of my dearly-loved grandson having thus been suddenly cut off in the flower of his age, full of promise for the future, amiable and gentle, and endearing himself to all, renders it hard for his sorely stricken parents, his dear young bride, and his fond grandmother to bow in submission to the inscrutable decrees of Providence.

"The sympathy of millions, which has been so touchingly and vividly expressed, is deeply gratifying at such a time, and I wish, both in my own name and that of my children, to express from my heart my warm gratitude to all.

"These testimonies of sympathy with us, and appreciation of my dear grandson, whom I loved as a son, and whose devotion to me was as great as that of a son, will be a help and consolation to me and mine in our affliction.

"My bereavements during the last thirty years of my reign have indeed been heavy. Though the labors, anxieties and responsibilities inseparable from my positon have been great, yet it is my earnest prayer that God may give me health and strength to work for the good and happiness of my dear country and Empire while life lasts.   VICTORIA, R. I."

Another deep shadow was thrown over the Queen and her family by the removal of one more of the company of Princes in the procession of 1887. Since his marriage in 1885, Prince Henry of Battenberg, the husband of Princess Beatrice, had been seldom away from the Court, whether at Windsor, Balmoral or Osborne, and had accompanied Her Majesty on her annual visits to the Continent in the spring. Adapting himself thoroughly to English life, ardently attached to the institutions and sports of the country, he had by his genial, courteous manner and unobtrusive tact won the affection of all with whom he was associated, and his bright presence is now sorely missed. Sprung from a family of soldiers, and brother of Prince Alexander, the hero of Slivnitza, it is not to be wondered at that, when a chance occurred of distinguishing himself in the field, he accepted it with eagerness, and volunteered for the expedition to Ashantee, which had just been organized. Throughout the march from the coast, Prince Henry proved his willingness to share the fatigue and labors of his comrades, and his presence was most useful in negotiations with native chiefs. The expedition had reached Kwisa, between Prahsu and Kumassi, the capital of King Prempeh, when the Prince was struck down by fever. He was promptly conveyed to the coast, and rallied after the journey. He embarked on board H. M. S. Blonde on the 17th of January in a weak state, and at one time seemed to regain strength. On the 19th, however, a change for the worst set in, and he passed peacefully away on the evening of January 20th, off the coast of Sierre Leone.

The sudden and tragic close of a life so bright and promising shocked the whole nation, and stirred to the depths their sympathies for the widow, for the fatherless children, and for the Queen. To Her Majesty, apart from its wholly unexpected character, the blow was the more severe, because, as her other children had been parted from her by the exigencies of their positions, she had learned to rely on her daughter's husband for that sympathy, support, and assistance which, as years passed on, became more valuable. In response to the universal expression of national feeling, Her Majesty wrote from Osborne on the 14th of February, 1896:

"I have, alas! once more to thank my loyal subjects for their warm sympathy in a fresh grievous affliction which has befallen me and my beloved daughter, Princess Beatrice, Princess Henry of Battenberg.

"This new sorrow is overwhelming, and to me is a double one, for I lose a dearly-beloved and helpful son, whose presence was like a bright sunbeam in my home, and my dear daughter loses a noble, devoted husband, to whom she was united by the closest affection.

"To witness the blighted happiness of the daughter who has never left me and has comforted and helped me, is hard to bear. But the feeling of universal sympathy so touchingly shown by all classes of my subjects has deeply moved my child and myself, and has helped and soothed us greatly. I wish from my heart to thank my people for this, as well as for the appreciation manifested of the dear and gallant Prince who laid down his life in the service of his adopted country.

"My beloved child is an example to all in her courage, resignation and submission to the will of God.

"VICTORIA, R. I."

The lamented Prince was, by his own wish, laid to rest at Whippingham, in the Isle of Wight, of which he had been Captain and Governor—an office which has since been conferred upon his widow. By her acceptance of this office Princess Henry showed, and it is but one proof among many, her courageous resolve not to allow her private sorrow to interfere with the performance of public duties.

On the 3d of May, 1893, the official announcement was made of the betrothal of the Duke of York, the only surviving son of the Prince and Princess of Wales, to the Princess Victoria Mary, only daughter of the Duke and Duchess of Teck. The marriage took place at St. James's Palace on the 6th of July, amid universal rejoicing, and never since the marriage of the Prince of Wales or the Queen's Jubilee procession had London been more thronged with loyal and enthusiastic crowds. The ceremony was performed by the Archbishop of Canterbury, in the presence of the Queen and all the royal family, with whom were the King and Queen of Denmark and the Czarevitch, now Emperor, of Russia. The bridesmaids were grandchildren and one great-grandchild of the Queen. After the rejoicings and congratulations from all parts of the Empire, the Queen addressed another letter to her people, in which she wrote of the universal loyalty shown to her. "It is, indeed, nothing new to the Queen, for in weal or woe she has ever met with the warmest, kindest sympathy, which she feels very deeply. She knows that the people of her vast Empire are aware how truly her heart beats for them in all their joys and sorrows, and that in the existence of this tie between them and herself lies the real strength of the Empire." The picture of the marriage ceremony, painted by command of the Queen by M. Tuxen, is reproduced overleaf.

The Duke and Duchess of York have now three children; the eldest,—a son—born on the 23d of June,

1894, has been christened Edward; the second,—also a son—named Albert, was born on December 14th, 1895; the third,—a daughter—named Victoria Alexandra Alice Mary, was born on April 25th, 1897. The name "Alice" commemorates the Grand Duchess of Hesse, and "Mary" the Duchess of Gloucester, on whose birthday the infant Princess was born. The descent of the crown in a direct line is thus, it is hoped, happily assured.

During the whole of her long life, in the midst of public business which has daily become more voluminous and exacting, the Queen has never entirely abandoned the pursits which were the pleasure and relaxation of her earliest years. Mention has been made of her practice of music and of her instructors, and here it may be noted that within the last fifteen years Her Majesty has sung with Signor Tosti, as at an earlier period she sang with Lablache and Mendelssohn. In all the extracts from the Queen's journals which have from time to time been made public, it will have been noticed how constantly she mentions that she sketched the scenery of the places visited by her. The early instruction, given by Westall and supplemented by the hints occasionally given by Sir E. Landseer, was not in landscape drawing, which was taught by Mr. Lear in 1846 and 1847. Since that time the Queen has taken lessons from Mr. Leitch, and within the last twelve years also from Mr. Green. The Queen has always followed with the closest interest the course of current events, which have necessarily absorbed the greater part of her time and attention. But Her Majesty has also made herself familiar with great imaginative writers, with poets such as Shakespeare, Scott and Tennyson, or with novelists such as Jane Austen, Charlotte Bronte, George Eliot, and it may be added, Mrs. Oliphant, whose recent illness and death aroused the Queen's deepest sympathy. The Queen's acquaintance with German and French literature is considerable, and her intimate knowledge of these languages is very noticeable in the purity with which she speaks them. In the last ten years a signal proof of the warm interest which Her Majesty has always taken in her Indian Empire has been given by the Queen's study of Hindustani, under the instruction of the Munshi Abdul Karim.

It is impossible to close this brief record of Her Majesty's life without mention of the memorable event of the 22nd of June, 1897. No such scene has ever been witnessed in any capital of the world as was afforded by London on that day, and throughout the whole Empire the commemoration of our Sovereign of Great Britain and Ireland was celebrated with a burst of enthusiasm absolutely without parallel.

The course to be followed by the State procession in going to and returning from St. Paul's Cathedral had been carefully planned, in order that the largest possible number of Her Majesty's subjects might be enabled to witness its passage through the streets. Eleven Prime Ministers of Colonial Houses of Representatives, accompanied by detachments of troops, whose presence from distant lands bore living witness to the extent and loyalty, of the Empire, preceded the procession through crowds of enthusiastic spectators. The Queen herself, accompanied by children, grandchildren, and great-grandchildren, escorted by cavalcades of Princes, and preceded by representatives accredited by every Foreign Power, and by troops drawn from all portions of a realm on which the sun never sets, passed slowly through the thronged and gaily-decorated streets to the Cathedral of St. Paul. There "Te Deum Laudamus" was sung with a genuine fervor of national thanksgiving for the prolongation of the life of a Sovereign, whose rule has fostered all that is best in the character of the British people, and throughout the world has ever made for peace. Before leaving Buckingham Palace Her Majesty sent to her subjects the message: "From my heart I thank my beloved people. May God bless them," which, in its adequacy and appropriateness, shows the perfect simplicity, womanly perception, and delicate tact, which has always enabled the Queen to strike the chord that vibrates through the heart of the nation.

In every town of Great Britain the occasion was celebrated with rejoicing, and the population of each city and village vied with each other in raising memorials of the event. In London and throughout the country the Prince of Wales took the lead in instituting a fund to defray the debts of the existing hospitals and to provide with more certainty for their future maintenance. Towards this object nearly a quarter of a million has been contributed, and this notwithstanding that half a million had been subscribed early in the year for the relief of the famished and plague-stricken natives of the East Indies. The Princess of Wales made the destitute population of London her care, and the letter written by her to the Lord Mayor of London met with such a hearty response that 300,000 of the poor of the metropolis took part in the rejoicings.

The magnificent fleet assembled at Spithead was reviewed, on the 26th of June, by the Prince of Wales on behalf of the Queen, who, to her deep regret, was unable, owing to the fatigue of the journey from Windsor, to be present in person. No finer fleet had ever been assembled in any waters, and the sight was the more impressive when it was known that this tremendous naval power was assembled without drawing upon the fleets, always in commission upon the seas, for one ship or one man. At Aldershot a large force of troops was reviewed by Her Majesty in person; 28,000 men of the British and Colonial troops, under the command of H. R. H. the Duke of Connaught, passed before the Queen, conspicuous among them being the Guards, the whole seven battalions forming this historic brigade being assembled together for the first time for forty years. The Queen afterwards held a special review of the Colonial contingent at Windsor. There also she received the 100 Bishops who had come to attend the Pan-Anglican Conference at Lambeth, the sixtieth anniversary of the Queen's reign being also the 1,300th anniversary of the conversion of Britain to Christianity.

From the Universities, and from all the great corporations and socieites, came deputations and addresses, all alike congratulating the Queen, and hoping that her beneficent rule might be still further prolonged. In answer the Queen published the following letter:—

"Windsor Castle, July 15th, 1897.

"I have frequently expressed my personal feelings to my people, and though on this memorable occasion there have been many official expressions of my deep sense of the unbounded loyalty evinced, I cannot rest satisfied without personally giving utterance to these sentiments.

"It is difficult for me on this occasion to say how truly touched and grateful I am for the spontaneous and

universal outburst of loyal attachment and real affection
which I have experienced on the completion of the Sixtieth year of my Reign.

"During my progress through London on June 22nd
this great enthusiasm was shown in the most striking
manner, and can never be effaced from my heart.

"It is indeed deeply gratifying, after so many years
of labor and anxiety for the good of my beloved Country, to find that my exertions have been appreciated
throughout my vast Empire.

"In weal and woe I have ever had the true sympathy of all my people, which has been warmly recipro-
cated by myself.

"It has given me unbounded pleasure to see so many
of my Subjects from all parts of the World assembled
here, and to find them joining in the acclamations of
loyal devotion to myself, and I would wish to thank them
all from the depth of my grateful heart.

"I shall ever pray God to bless them and to enable
me still to discharge my duties for their welfare as long
as life lasts.   VICTORIA, R. I."

Limits of space have excluded all but the most in-
cidental allusions to salient events of Her Majesty's
reign. Scarcely any reference has been made to constitutional changes which have peacefully effected a vast
transference of political power, and yet, through the wisdom of the Sovereign, have only served to strengthen the
British Monarchy. In like manner the enormous growth
of the Empire has been barely mentioned, an Empire
which, in spite of varieites of race, language and climate,
in spite also of differences of constitutions and creeds
and customs, has been welded into unexampled unity by

the tie of personal loyalty to Queen Victoria. Nothing
has been said of the religious forces which have added,
at home and abroad, new chapters to the romance of spir-
itual chivalry, and enriched and purified the springs of
national life; of the poets, novelists, historians, and artists who have added the lustre of their genius to the
Victorian era; of the achievements of science, which has
opened up new worlds of thought, revolutionized the
arts alike of peace and war, ameliorated the conditions of
existence, and lightened the burden of suffering; of the
spread of education, which has given to millions the
means of acquiring the knowledge that was once the possession only of the few. Nothing, finally, has been said
of the material progress of the nation, of the revolution
effected by the application of steam to manufacture and
locomotion, or of the social and industrial problems,
which rapid changes have set for our solution. Yet we
might trust with confidence that such difficulties would
be conquered, if, in future generations, all those who
direct the counsels of the realm are as just, as prudent, as
laborious, as unselfish, as permeated with love of country,
as profoundly interested in the true well-being of the lab-
oring classes, as Queen Victoria.

Lightning Source UK Ltd.
Milton Keynes UK
UKOW06n2232131216
289913UK00001B/59/P